awesome

8

EPIC

GALENA PUBLIC LIBRARY DISTRICT

D1486922

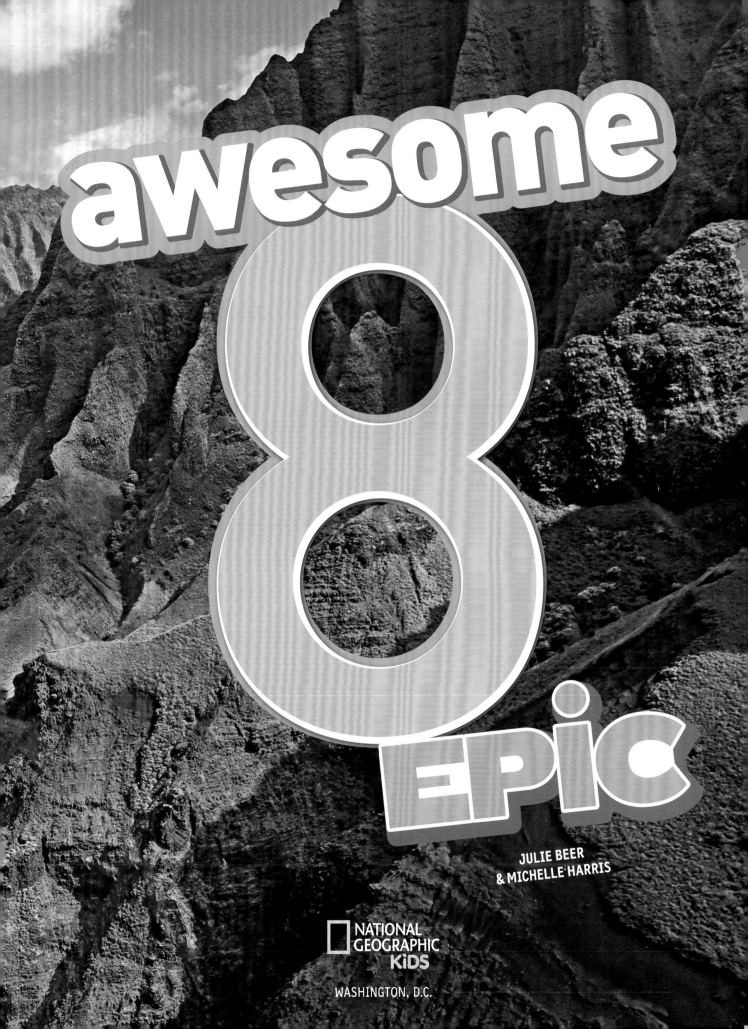

awesome 8

EPIC

JULIE BEER
& MICHELLE HARRIS

NATIONAL
GEOGRAPHIC
KiDS

WASHINGTON, D.C.

HEY THERE, AWESOME READERS!

ARE YOU READY ...

... to check out some of the most epic animals, adventures, and attractions on Earth? Well, you've picked up the right book! *Awesome 8 Epic* takes you all over the world in its quest for the very coolest of, well, everything. Let's get started!

WHAT IS *AWESOME 8 EPIC*?

Awesome 8 Epic is a picture-packed list book featuring the wildest, wackiest, and most mind-blowing things we could think of.

WHY EIGHT?

Why *not* eight? Oh—you mean, why not a top ten list, instead? Well, eight is a little more exclusive than ten—meaning things have to be even *more* amazing to make the cut!

DO I HAVE TO START AT THE BEGINNING?

Definitely not! Pick up the book, flip to a page that catches your eye, and dive in! You can always go back to the topics you skipped.

WHAT ELSE IS IN THIS BOOK?

Awesome 8 Epic features sensational spreads showcasing everything from the oddest deep-sea creatures to the strangest sky sensations, from the speediest sports to the craziest caves. Along the way are fantastically fun facts and stories where we dig deeper into some of the creatures, technology, and places featured.

ANYTHING ELSE I SHOULD KNOW?

Yes! There are some pretty awesome activities described in this book, but please don't try ANYTHING without first consulting an adult. Safety first, Awesome 8'ers. Now turn the page and jump on in!

TABLE OF CONTENTS

EIGHT UNBELIEVABLE ANIMAL IMAGES

GET READY TO DO A DOUBLE TAKE. THESE CRITTERS KNOW HOW TO MUG FOR THE CAMERA!

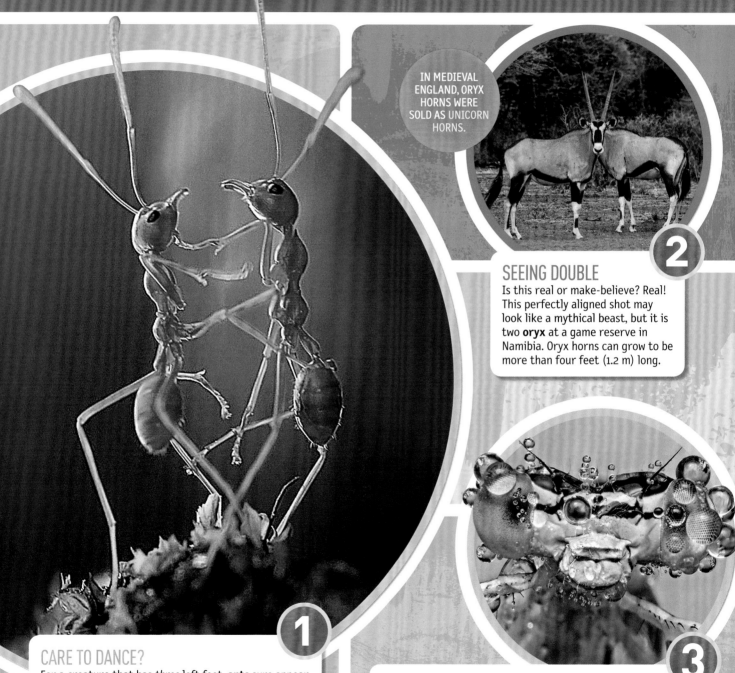

IN MEDIEVAL ENGLAND, ORYX HORNS WERE SOLD AS UNICORN HORNS.

SEEING DOUBLE

Is this real or make-believe? Real! This perfectly aligned shot may look like a mythical beast, but it is two **oryx** at a game reserve in Namibia. Oryx horns can grow to be more than four feet (1.2 m) long.

CARE TO DANCE?

For a creature that has *three* left feet, **ants** sure appear to be good dancers! Actually, this is just a well-timed photo of two ants greeting each other. It took 150 shots snapped in the backyard of the photographer's East Java, Indonesia, home to capture this winner.

BUG-EYED

Here's looking at you! A Slovakian photographer captures **insects** doused in water droplets with a macro lens, revealing the burden these creatures carry when they get wet. His photos are usually taken in the wild with morning dew or after a rainstorm.

HAPPY FACE SPIDERS ARE ONE OF VERY FEW SPIDERS THAT CARE FOR THEIR YOUNG AFTER THEY'RE BORN.

5 BREAKFAST FOR TWO

Don't mind if I do! These two curious **giraffes** are popping in for a snack at Giraffe Manor, a hotel in Nairobi, Kenya, where giraffes roam the grounds and visit guests through the dining rooms' windows!

4 ALL SMILES

Here's a spider guaranteed to bring a smile to your face. The **happy face spider** was named for—you guessed it!—its unique markings. Found in Hawaiian rain forests, it's just one-quarter of an inch (6 mm) long and not harmful to people.

6 UP A TREE

Money doesn't grow on trees, but it sure looks like these **goats** do! As many as a dozen goats routinely climb the 30-foot (9.1-m)-tall argan trees in southwestern Morocco to eat the fruit and leaves.

7 SAY "CHEESE!"

Is this my good side? These two playful **foxes** got their paws on a photographer's camera at a national park in Vienna, Austria. After leaving out some treats and watching nearby from a tent, the photographer took these photos of the pair having a field day with his equipment.

8 THAT TICKLES!

Check out this all-natural butterfly crown! An Australian scientist caught this butterfly-covered **caiman** lounging on a log in southeastern Peru. These reptiles, which are related to alligators, live on the edges of rivers and streams in Central and South America.

Hi-High-Altitude ADVENTURES

A FEAR OF HEIGHTS IS A DEAL BREAKER IF YOU WANT TO TACKLE ANY OF THESE HIGH-ADRENALINE SPORTS.

2

WHERE'S THE BEACH?

Skysurfers take their boards to the skies. Jumping from a plane with a parachute on their back and a board strapped to their feet, they perform tricks, spins, and twists during their free fall to Earth.

1

REACHING NEW HEIGHTS

Extreme skier Andrea Binning got a lift from a helicopter to make this epic run down a mountain in Alaska, U.S.A. As opposed to using a ski lift, **heli-skiing** means getting dropped off at remote sites to ski down uncharted territory, not on groomed trails.

EIGHT MILLION PEOPLE WATCHED BAUMGARTNER'S JUMP LIVE ONLINE.

5

WATCH YOUR STEP

In 2012, Felix Baumgartner **jumped** 127,852 feet (38,969 m) from a helium-filled balloon in space and fell back to Earth, reaching a speed of 843.6 miles an hour (1,357.6 km/h). Wearing a parachute to break his fall, he touched ground in about 4 minutes and 20 seconds. That's one giant leap!

8

WINGING IT

Perhaps the most adrenaline-fueled sport is also one of the most dangerous. **Wingsuit fliers** wear nylon jumpsuits that mimic the skin flaps of a flying squirrel. Fabric stretches between the fliers' arms and legs and between their feet. Then they jump off a cliff and glide before opening a parachute to land.

4

IN SOUTH AFRICA, ZIP LINES ARE CALLED FOEFIE SLIDES.

ZIPPING ALONG

This adventurer is looking down at South Africa's landscape while harnessed into a **zip line**. Whether gliding through rain forests, cityscapes, or river gorges, the thrill of zip lines is all about speed, height, and distance. The world's longest zip line stretches for more than a mile (1.6 km)!

7

JUST HANGING AROUND

As if **trapeze** weren't extreme enough, aerial artist Anna Cochrane took to the skies and did it while hanging from a hot air balloon! Cochrane performed her fantastic feat at an elevation of 10,365 feet (3,159 m) while suspended above the east coast of the South Island of New Zealand.

3

BABY STEPS

Talk about a balancing act! In Rio de Janeiro, Brazil, **highlining** is a popular sport for thrill-seekers. A rope is anchored between two points at least 33 feet (10 m) above the ground, and the brave (who are usually harnessed in) walk across—sometimes in shoes, sometimes not.

6

TOP OF THE WORLD

Climbing to the top of Earth's highest mountain is no walk in the park. Besides the physical training, most climbers spend several months at lower base camps to get used to the high altitude before they conquer Mount Everest's peak. Ever since it was first summited, in 1953, more than 4,000 people have made it to the 29,029-foot (8,848-m) summit.

Fantastic FOOD MASH-UPS

AN EVERYDAY FOOD + ANOTHER EVERYDAY FOOD = SOME UNEXPECTEDLY WILD CREATIONS!

ONE STORE THAT SELLS SUSHI DOUGH-NUTS CALLS THEM DOSHI.

A HOLE IN ONE

These "doughnuts" are a little fishy! **Sushi doughnuts** are sushi rolls in which rice is pressed into a doughnut mold and traditional "toppings" like spicy tuna, cucumber, and avocado are added on top. Chopsticks are optional.

①

POULTRY OVERLOAD

To make a **turducken**, take a stuffed chicken and put it inside a stuffed duck and put all of that inside a stuffed turkey. (And if you eat it, you'll probably be pretty stuffed yourself!) The dish is said to have originated in Louisiana, U.S.A., more than 30 years ago.

2

3

THREE'S A CROWD

Can't decide what flavor pie you want? Order a **cherpumple** and you can have them all! A cherpumple is made of a cherry pie baked into a white cake, a pumpkin pie baked into a spice cake, and an apple pie baked into a yellow cake—all stacked on top of one another and frosted as one dessert. Yum!

4

A PUMPE-CAPPLE USES PUMPKIN, PECAN, AND APPLE PIES.

GOT MILK?

Can't decide whether you want a brownie or a cookie? Grab a **brookie**! This sweet combo is basically a brownie with a cookie baked on top of it, but the flavor possibilities are endless. The type of cookie can vary—from chocolate chip to snickerdoodle—and the brownie can be chocolate or cocoa-free (made with white chocolate or butterscotch chips). Dig in!

5

CRAZED FOR CRONUTS

The Cronut is a **croissant crossed with a doughnut** with some extras. It's rolled in sugar, filled with cream, and dipped in a glaze. A New York City pastry chef first started selling Cronuts in 2013, and long lines immediately formed with customers eager to buy the $5.75 treat.

IT TAKES THREE DAYS TO MAKE A CRONUT.

6

WHICH CAME FIRST?

This is one time you *should* put all your eggs in one basket. Take a basic meat loaf recipe and put half the mixture in a pan. Then place whole, hard-boiled eggs down the center end to end and cover with the other half of the mixture. Bake and slice to "hatch" an awesomely unusual **egg meatloaf.**

8

7

NO-MESS SPAGHETTI

Imagine eating spaghetti without all the splatters. Enter the **spaghetti sandwich**—a finger-licking hybrid that combines spaghetti and marinara sauce with some melted cheese, all rolled up inside a sandwich. Now that's one-stop dining!

WHOA, THAT'S NUTS

Wonuts are two breakfasts in one! Take basic doughnut dough, pour it in a waffle iron, and—voilà!—you've got a **wonut.** Wonuts can be topped with doughnut favorites, like sprinkles and nuts, or eaten hot off the press.

TURN THE PAGE TO FILL UP ON MORE FOOD FUN!

MORE THAN MEETS THE EYE

YOUR TASTE BUDS ARE JUST ONE OF THE MANY INFLUENCES ON HOW YOU FEEL ABOUT YOUR FOOD. YOUR EYES, NOSE, AND EVEN YOUR MEMORY PLAY IMPORTANT PARTS, TOO.

A perfectly plated dish—with colorful garnish, a swirl of sauce, and superbly sprinkled spices—can get your brain thinking how tasty the food is going to be before you even dig in. On the other hand, a gloppy stew in an unattractive bowl with splatters on the edges may not send your tummy grumbling. How come? Even though you might assume sight has nothing to do with taste, it turns out that what we see can change our perception of how things taste.

In one study, participants were asked to drink a cherry-flavored drink that had been tinted orange. Instead of guessing that the drink they were tasting was cherry, most taste-testers thought it was orange or fruit-punch flavored. They not only assumed the drink was the flavor they associated with the color of the drink, they thought they were tasting it, too!

Humans can detect five basic tastes: sweet, sour, salty, bitter, and savory. Taste receptors inside our taste buds on our tongue and the roof of our mouth send a signal to our brain, which recognizes these tastes the moment we put something in our mouth. Then we quickly make the "yum!" or "eww!" response. We also have sensory cells in our mouth that pick up temperature and texture. Clearly, there is a lot going on with taste that we can't see, too.

And then there's smell. If you've ever tried holding your nose while you eat something, you know that it can dull the flavor. Your sense of smell is so tied to food that when you smell a burger on a grill you associate that smell with how the burger tastes.

Another important part of taste is your memory. If you have happy memories of eating a dish at your grandma's house over the winter holidays, you may immediately like the same dish that's put in front of you no matter how it looks or where you're eating it.

EIGHT BONKERS BURGERS

1
WHAT: Ramen Burger
WHY IT'S UNUSUAL: Boiled ramen noodles are shaped into a bun and fried.

2
WHAT: Peanut Butter Cup Burger
WHY IT'S UNUSUAL: This burger is topped with peanut butter cups (and bacon and fried onions).

3
WHAT: Doughnut Burger
WHY IT'S UNUSUAL: You can have your breakfast with your lunch when doughnuts double as buns.

4
WHAT: Gobble Gobble Burger
WHY IT'S UNUSUAL: Celebrate Thanksgiving every day. This turkey burger includes cranberry sauce, gravy, and even macaroni and cheese bites!

WHAT: Mac and Cheese Burger ⑤
WHY IT'S UNUSUAL: Who needs a cheeseburger when you can have a mac and cheese burger? (That's a regular burger with a scoop of mac and cheese.)

WHAT: Waffleburger ⑥
WHY IT'S UNUSUAL: Bread is ordinary. Why not eat a burger between two waffles instead?

WHAT: Lasagna Burger ⑦
WHY IT'S UNUSUAL: Two meals in one: a burger on a roll with lasagna noodles, pasta sauce, and cheese!

WHAT: Haystack Burger ⑧
WHY IT'S UNUSUAL: This big burger included 40 ounces (1.1 kg) of beef, bacon, onions, cheese, and coleslaw!

EIGHT
HIGHLY UNUSUAL
CANVASES
THESE ARTISTS KNOW HOW TO THINK OUTSIDE THE BOX.

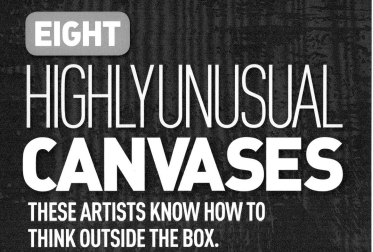

GAME POINT!

1

In Cape Town, South Africa, **embroidery artist** Danielle Clough restrung this racquet in an eye-catching way. Using vintage tennis and badminton racquets as her canvas, her embroidery patterns include everything from plants to flowers to birds. She sometimes even embroiders on fences!

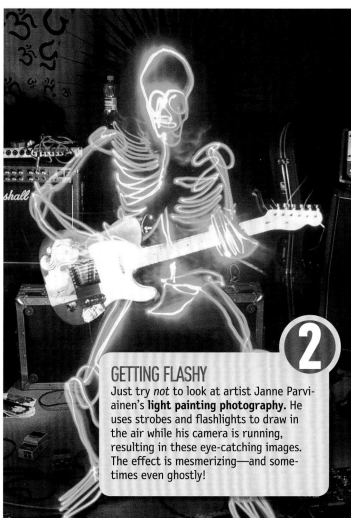

GETTING FLASHY

2

Just try *not* to look at artist Janne Parviainen's **light painting photography.** He uses strobes and flashlights to draw in the air while his camera is running, resulting in these eye-catching images. The effect is mesmerizing—and sometimes even ghostly!

EGG-CELLENT PORTRAITS

There's one thing that Barak Hardley's portraits have in common: They're all **egg heads!** The California, U.S.A.-based artist paints famous people—real and fictional—onto eggs every Easter, though he starts planning his egg-ceptional creations months ahead of time.

POSH PASTA

Get your veggies with a side of rainbow! These argyle **lasagna noodles** are made by Linda Miller Nicholson, a chef in Seattle, Washington, U.S.A., using peas, parsley, beets, and herbs— no artificial dyes.

4

SOME PEOPLE ONCE THOUGHT PUTTING MASHED PUMPKIN ON THEIR FACE WOULD GET RID OF THEIR FRECKLES.

HEAR ME ROAR

5

The lion doesn't just sleep tonight—it glows! This king of the jungle **pumpkin** was on display at the Jack-O'-Lantern Spectacular in Louisville, Kentucky, U.S.A. Every year, some 5,000 illuminated pumpkins line a 1,500-foot (457-m)-long trail; more than 100 are carved into works of art.

NAILED IT!

This **fingernail art** is frighteningly good! Detailed nail art may seem trendy, but painting nails has actually been in vogue for thousands of years. Ancient Babylonians painted their nails before they went into battle. And during China's Ming dynasty, nails were decorated using beeswax, egg whites, and vegetable dyes.

7

ONLY THE HIGHEST-RANKING ANCIENT EGYPTIANS WERE ALLOWED TO WEAR RED NAIL POLISH.

FOOD AS ART

6

You might want to take a photo before you clean this plate. In London, England, after food photographer Lauren Purnell prepares a meal, she uses the leftover scraps of fruits and veggies to make a **"culinary canvas."** There's no food waste, and what's left is art.

FANCY FOAM

8

This latte is certain to give you a serious milk mustache! Carefully sculpted milk froth can take the form of everything from hearts to leaves to pandas. At the annual World **Latte Art** Championship, coffee artists hand-pour their designs—no tools or etching allowed!

EIGHT
BRILLIANT BRIDGES

FROM ROPE BRIDGES TO ULTRAMODERN SPANS, THESE EIGHT ARCHITECTURAL WONDERS STRETCH ENGINEERING LIMITS. GET READY TO HOLD ON TO THE GUARDRAILS!

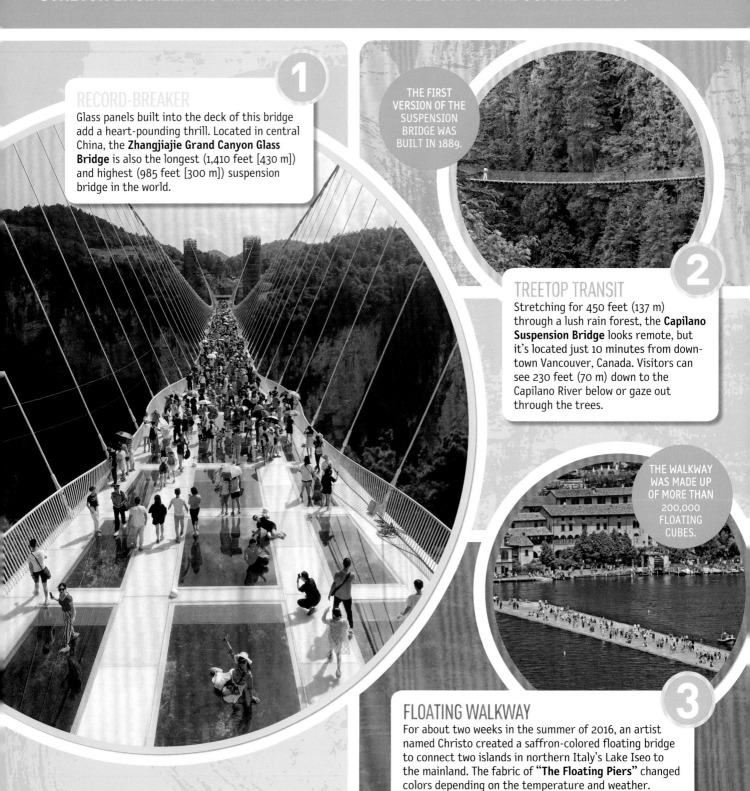

1 RECORD-BREAKER

Glass panels built into the deck of this bridge add a heart-pounding thrill. Located in central China, the **Zhangjiajie Grand Canyon Glass Bridge** is also the longest (1,410 feet [430 m]) and highest (985 feet [300 m]) suspension bridge in the world.

THE FIRST VERSION OF THE SUSPENSION BRIDGE WAS BUILT IN 1889.

2 TREETOP TRANSIT

Stretching for 450 feet (137 m) through a lush rain forest, the **Capilano Suspension Bridge** looks remote, but it's located just 10 minutes from downtown Vancouver, Canada. Visitors can see 230 feet (70 m) down to the Capilano River below or gaze out through the trees.

THE WALKWAY WAS MADE UP OF MORE THAN 200,000 FLOATING CUBES.

3 FLOATING WALKWAY

For about two weeks in the summer of 2016, an artist named Christo created a saffron-colored floating bridge to connect two islands in northern Italy's Lake Iseo to the mainland. The fabric of **"The Floating Piers"** changed colors depending on the temperature and weather.

STEEL SAILS

4

Peeking above low clouds, the **Øresund Bridge** soars more than 1,600 feet (490 m) over the Flint Channel to connect Malmö, Sweden, to Copenhagen, Denmark. The cable-stayed bridge carries cars on the upper level and trains on the lower.

WAVY WONDER

5

This bridge knows how to make a splash! The **Henderson Waves** bridge in Singapore is made from balau wood, found only in Southeast Asia. The twists crest for 900 feet (274 m) to offer walkers hidden hiding spots. Its wavy form shines at dusk.

FLYING FOOTBRIDGE

6

When completed in 2000, the **Millennium Footbridge** became the first walkway built over the Thames River in central London, England, in more than a hundred years. This 1,210-foot (370-m)-long steel bridge was destroyed in the movie *Harry Potter and the Half-Blood Prince*—but don't worry, that was all done by special effects.

WILLIAM SHAKE-SPEARE'S GLOBE THEATER IS LOCATED ON THE SOUTH SIDE OF THE FOOTBRIDGE.

RENAISSANCE MARVEL

7

This bridge took almost 500 years to build—sort of. Renaissance artist **Leonardo da Vinci** designed the bridge for a sultan, but it was never built. When completed in 2001 near Oslo, Norway, the wooden pedestrian bridge brought Leonardo da Vinci's design to life.

ON THE ROPES

8

Look down (if you dare!) at Northern Ireland's windswept, rocky coast when crossing the gently swaying **Carrick-a-Rede Rope Bridge.** Fishermen crafted the bridge—which is now made of wire-rope and Douglas fir—350 years ago to reach migrating salmon.

THE ICEMAN COMETH

1

In 1991, hikers in the Alps on the border between Austria and Italy stumbled upon a remarkable relic: **Ötzi**, a 5,300-year-old mummy also known as the "Iceman." Into his icy grave Ötzi carried Neolithic artifacts, including a copper axe and two arrows.

ANALYSIS OF ÖTZI'S STOMACH CONTENTS SHOWED HE HAD JUST EATEN A LARGE MEAL OF WILD GOAT.

EIGHT
STUNNING MUMMIES

NO NEED TO FEAR A CURSE FROM THESE MAGNIFICENT MUMMIES

FANTASTIC FIND

2

Archaeologist Zahi Hawass examines Tomb 54 in the **Valley of the Golden Mummies,** located in Bahariya oasis, around 300 miles (480 km) from Cairo, Egypt. Discovered in 1996, the four tombs here contain more than 200 beautifully preserved mummies that are more than 2,300 years old.

THE MUMMIES WERE FOUND WHEN A DONKEY TRIPPED ON THE EDGE OF A TOMB.

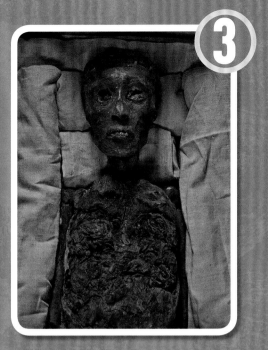

(3) BOY KING

When teenage **King Tutankhamun** died in 1322 B.C., his death threw Egypt into chaos. But the 1922 discovery of his tomb, and the mummy within, caused its own kind of commotion: Tut became a worldwide sensation.

(4) SECRET CRYPT

A 1994 church renovation in **Vác, Hungary,** led to the rediscovery of a group of mummies hidden in a secret crypt. The bodies—including that of this local man who died in 1806—mummified naturally in the cool, dry air.

(5) CROCODILE GOD

Nearly 2,000 years old, this embalmed crocodile shows the ancient Egyptian devotion to the god **Sobek,** who was represented by the head of a crocodile and the body of a man. Sobek, the god of the River Nile, had one mighty duty: He protected the king.

(6) SOUTH AMERICAN MUMMIES

The **Chinchorro** lived thousands of years ago along the coasts of what is today Peru and Chile. The ancient group mummified everyone, including children, as shown here. Bodies were stuffed with straw, grasses, and pastes made from ash and water.

(7) GOOD LUCK KITTY

Thousands of years ago, ancient Egyptians **mummified cats,** birds, crocodiles, and other animals. Salt was rubbed into their bodies to make sure the animals dried out. Mummified felines were offered to the gods for good luck.

(8) SURPRISE INSIDE

A CT scan of a **Buddha statue** led to an unusual surprise. Contained inside the statue was a nearly 1,000-year-old mummy of a Buddhist monk! Self-mummification was a complicated process that involved the monk eating a special diet of bark, nuts, seeds, berries, and fruits for months beforehand.

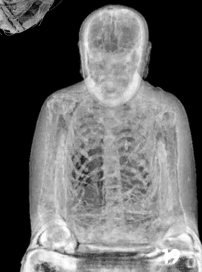

EIGHT MINI-GOLF COURSES THAT ARE ON PAR

WHETHER YOU PREFER MOVABLE ROOFTOP ADVENTURES, AN ERUPTING VOLCANO, OR A QUIET NOOK WHERE YOU CAN READ A BOOK, THESE COURSES HAVE YOU COVERED.

1 CLUB CAR

If the weather turns sour, the owners of this rooftop, four-par mini-golf course can just drive to sunnier skies. Two British friends created the crazy **cartop course,** with its movable putting green ... but we have no idea why.

2 BOOK BIRDIE

With greens made of carpet and sand traps made of books, the Kennebunk Free Library in Kennebunk, Maine, U.S.A., transformed the **library's aisles** into an 18-hole mini-golf course as a "par-fect" fund-raiser to help keep the library going strong.

3 OVERHEAD TRAFFIC

There's no peace and quiet on this course! Under a busy **freeway** in Tokyo, Japan, golfers putt on greens that provide a splash of color and make the most of what is usually wasted space.

SHINING BRIGHT

 4

Black light adds a new dimension to sinking your putts at this course in Brussels, Belgium. Black light, which emits a longer wavelength than visible light, makes white objects like T-shirts and teeth glow.

SHOPPING SENSATION

5

A cartoon world comes to life at the 18-hole **Professor Wem's Adventure Golf,** in the West Edmonton Mall in Alberta, Canada. The mall also has an underground aquarium with more than a hundred species, including penguins and sea turtles.

HAWAII'S KĪLAUEA VOLCANO HAS BEEN CONSTANTLY, AND SLOWLY, ERUPTING SINCE 1983.

ERUPTING WITH FUN

7

There's always a threat of an eruption at the **Hawaiian Rumble** miniature golf course in North Myrtle Beach, South Carolina, U.S.A. The course brings a Hawaiian feel to the East Coast with a 40-foot (12-m)-tall volcano that rumbles three times an hour.

RAIN FOREST QUEST

6

Adventurers at this course in Herndon, Virginia, U.S.A., aren't just on the hunt for a hole in one. They're also on the lookout for Percy Fawcett, a British explorer who ventured into the Amazon in the 1920s looking for a lost city—never to be seen again. **Animated butterflies** and around 20 other characters bring the rain forest to life.

8

SLIP AND SLIDE

Passengers on **Carnival's *Triumph* cruise ship** take time out from deck-side R&R to sink a few putts on its mini-golf course. The ship leaves from New Orleans, Louisiana, U.S.A., to travel the Caribbean, where ocean-going putts are par for this course.

AN OCTOPUS'S ARMS CAN THINK INDEPENDENTLY FROM ITS BRAIN.

SNEAKY SMARTS

①

Octopuses are curious creatures. They can open the lids of jars, and some have even found escape routes from their aquarium enclosures, wriggling their boneless bodies through passages as small as a quarter. They learn quickly and can even recognize individual human faces.

EIGHT Incredibly Clever CREATURES

THESE ANIMALS AREN'T JUST ADORABLE AND CHARMING, THEY'RE AT THE TOP OF THEIR CLASS IN SMARTS!

② THIRST FOR KNOWLEDGE

Chimpanzees, one of the closest relatives to humans, have been seen using leaves and moss like sponges to soak up water for drinking. They pass on this trick to other family members, which is a type of social learning reserved for the smartest of animals.

CRAFTY CROW

④

If a **New Caledonian crow** can't find a tool for the job, it just makes one! The South Pacific bird has been observed bending twigs into hooks to get at insects hidden in logs. Now that's crafty!

⑤ NO BIRDBRAIN!

AN AFRICAN GRAY PARROT NAMED ALEX COULD RECOGNIZE COLORS AND SHAPES.

African gray parrots are known for being chatterboxes. They are excellent at mimicking humans and can even form simple sentences. But they are also one of a few animals that are capable of reasoning. They're able to figure out puzzles and even work together to problem-solve. Brainy birds!

③ ALL FOR ONE

Talk about teamwork! These **army ants** in Panama are joining together to build a living ant bridge, while a few individuals cross over to bring food to their nest. Researchers have discovered that no single ant calls the shots in the bridge-building; they make calculated decisions as a colony.

NUTS FOR LEARNING

⑥

When it comes to finding nuts, **gray squirrels** are all business. In one study, researchers hid hazelnuts to measure how squirrels solved a puzzle. The squirrels proved to be quick learners, used reasoning, and even changed tactics to get their nut reward more quickly.

⑧ BRIGHT AND BUBBLY

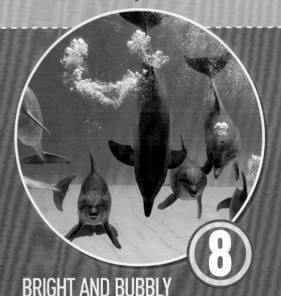

Being playful is a sign of intelligence—which puts **dolphins** near the top of the list of the smartest animals. Dolphins are known to ride the waves of fishing boats, and captive dolphins have been seen blowing bubbles from their blowholes and then swimming through them!

TURN THE PAGE FOR MORE ON DOLPHIN SMARTS!

SMART LITTLE PIGGY

⑦

They may like to wallow in mud, but **domestic pigs** clean up in the intelligence department. They can learn tasks, like operating levers to get food, and are one of a select group of animals that understand how mirrors work.

DOLPHIN SMARTS

RESOURCEFUL, COOPERATIVE, AND CLEVER: DOLPHINS ARE THE SMARTY-PANTS OF THE RIVERS, LAKES, AND SEAS.

DOLPHINS CAN SHUT DOWN HALF OF THEIR BRAIN TO GO TO SLEEP AND STILL USE THE OTHER HALF TO STAY ALERT FOR PREDATORS!

They may not make the honor roll at your school, but bottlenose dolphins are pretty smart. They have larger brains than humans and have a greater brain-to-body-weight ratio—a way scientists measure intelligence—than great apes. And after dolphins learn something, they are able to pass that knowledge on to other dolphins! That kind of intelligence is not typical in the animal kingdom.

When they are wide awake, dolphins are very social. As soon as they're born, they squawk, whistle, click, and squeak to communicate with one another. Scientists believe they communicate about everything from sharing where the good fishing spots are to warning one another of sharks in the area. Dolphins can recognize the signature whistles of other dolphins, even if they haven't crossed paths in as long as 20 years!

Dolphins are also famously playful. They have been seen playing a version of tag, where one dolphin nudges another indicating they want to play, then they both take off, chasing each other in turn. These social butterflies are also capable of solving problems by working together. Researchers in the United States gave a locked canister filled with fish to captive dolphins. The only way to open the canister was to pull a rope at each end of the canister at the same time, which required a group effort. The dolphins were repeatedly successful, capable of opening the canister in 30 seconds!

Not only are dolphins clever, they're also crafty and resourceful: They know how to use tools. This is unusual for animals and is considered a marker of higher intelligence. In Australia, some dolphins put marine sponges on their beaks to protect themselves from scrapes while scouring the ocean floor for prey.

EIGHT SUPERB SPECIES OF DOLPHINS …

① **Amazon River Dolphin** These dolphins, also known as pink dolphins, live only in freshwater rivers and lakes of South America.

② **Orca** Orcas (also called killer whales) often hunt in pods of up to 40 family members.

③ **Peale's Dolphin** Found off the coast of South America, Peale's dolphins swim in kelp beds and eat squid and octopus.

④ **Pygmy Killer Whale** These dolphins are often seen "logging"—resting in groups at the surface of the water, all facing the same direction.

⑤ **Spinner Dolphin** The name says it all: These high-energy dolphins spin when they leap out of the water! They can reach heights of 9.8 feet (3 m) and sometimes travel in groups of more than 1,000!

⑥ **Atlantic Humpback Dolphin** Found off the coast of West Africa, Atlantic humpbacks have been known to drive schools of fish toward shore and straight into fishermen's nets.

⑦ **Heaviside's Dolphin** One of the smallest dolphin species, they cruise alongside boats off of southwestern Africa and sometimes do somersaults up to 6.6 feet (2 m) in the air!

⑧ **Southern Right Whale Dolphin** These slow-swimming dolphins found in Southern Hemisphere waters sometimes do headstands, turning upside down with their flukes (tails) waving in the air.

EIGHT STRANGEST

STRANGEST

THE SKY IS THE LIMIT WITH THESE INCREDIBLE ATMOSPHERIC PHENOMENA.

SKY SENSATIONS

HELLO, HALO

When light is refracted and reflected by millions of ice crystals in high cirrus clouds, a ring around the sun (or moon) can form. Scientists call these solar or lunar rings **22-degree halos,** because the ring has a radius of about—you guessed it—22 degrees around the sun (or moon). That's one radical ring!

2

OUR SOLAR SYSTEM IS LOCATED ABOUT TWO-THIRDS FROM THE MILKY WAY'S CENTER.

NORTHERN LIGHTS

1

The **aurora borealis** brings vivid green swirls to Jökulsárlón, a glacial lagoon in southeast Iceland. When charged particles from the sun hit oxygen molecules about 60 miles (100 km) above Earth, they excite the atoms to give off the stunning green glow.

STARRY SKY

3

A long exposure taken of the **Milky Way** over the Black Sea shows off our home galaxy. All the stars we can see from Earth are in the Milky Way, and astronomers estimate that our galaxy has 100 to 400 billion stars in it.

RED BOW

5

A beautiful red arch frames the town of Terrassa, Spain. These unusual **rainbows** form when the sun is very low in the sky. The shorter wavelengths of green and blue light are scattered by air and dust particles, and the remaining light is full of reds.

EXTRATERRESTRIAL CLOUDS

4

These striking clouds may look like flying saucers, but their origins have a more earthly explanation. **Lenticular clouds** often form when moist air flows over a mountain and the crest of the wave of air cools enough to create these unusual formations.

OMINOUS CUMULONIMBUS

6

A dramatic thunderstorm cloud swirls above a grassy plain. Cumulonimbus clouds and these powerful storm systems form at less than 6,500 feet (1,980 m) in altitude during hot, humid weather. Powerful updrafts in **supercell clouds** can spawn violent storms and tornadoes.

SUPER STUNNER

7

A **supermoon** glows orange behind the Lincoln Memorial in Washington, D.C. You can see a supersize moon when the full-moon stage of the lunar cycle coincides with the moon's closest approach to Earth. Astronomers call this a perigee full moon.

EYE IN THE SKY

8

As seen from space, Hurricane Erin churns in the Atlantic Ocean in September 2001. A **hurricane's** defined eye (seen here as the blue sky in the center of the white swirl) contains light winds and fair weather, but the wall (the edges around the eye) is the area with the hurricane's highest winds.

1 LIGHT METER

The slits in domestic **cats'** eyes give them their distinct look, but they're also highly functional. Cats are active both day and night, and their eyes can adjust to all light settings. Their pupils become round to let in lots of light and become slits to let in less light.

EIGHT PECULIAR PEEPERS

HERE'S LOOKING AT YOU! SEEING IS BELIEVING WITH THESE WILD AND WEIRD ANIMAL EYES.

2 KEEP AN EYE OUT

Not only do **goats** have horizontal rectangular-shaped pupils, they are able to rotate their peepers 50 degrees—10 times more than humans—to keep those slits parallel with the ground. This helps them spot predators while they're grazing.

BUG-EYED

The majority of a **dragonfly's** head is made up of its eyes. Those prominent peepers allow it to see nearly everything around it except what's happening directly in the rear. And, if that's not enough, they can distinguish between colors better than humans.

4

TARSIERS' EARS MOVE INDEPENDENTLY OF EACH OTHER, WHICH HELPS THEM LOCATE PREY.

3 — ALL-SEEING EYE

There is no sneaking up on a **chameleon:** This remarkable reptile has eyes on the back of its head! Well, practically, anyway. It has almost 360-degree vision, meaning it can rotate and focus its eyes independently of each other and is able to look at two different things at the same time!

WHAT BIG EYES YOU HAVE

A **tarsier's** eyes are bigger than its brain! This primate—which can fit in a human hand—is nocturnal, so its enormous eyes help it see well at night. This miniature mammal's eyes are fixed in its skull, but its head can turn 180 degrees to check out what's happening in its Asian forest habitat.

5

EYE SEE YOU

An eye the size of a soccer ball had better win you the title of biggest eye of any animal on the planet. The **giant squid** wins that competition hands down! Its big eyes help the deep-sea cephalopod look out for its top predator: the sperm whale.

WHERE ARE MY SHADES?

6

Don't ever challenge a **gecko** to a staring contest: They'll win every time! These lizards can't blink, because they don't have eyelids. Most have big bulgy eyes with vertical pupils, like some snakes. Because they can't close their eyes when it's bright outside, geckos' pupils shrink to narrow slits to protect their eyes from sunrays.

7

A LITTLE SHIFTY

8

An **octopus's** unique dumbbell-shaped pupil has a purpose beyond just looking cool. It allows light to enter the lens from all different directions, helping them detect color. But their eyes aren't the only things doing the seeing: Some octopuses' skin can also detect light, which may explain why they are so good at camouflage.

OCTOPUSES DON'T HAVE A BLIND SPOT.

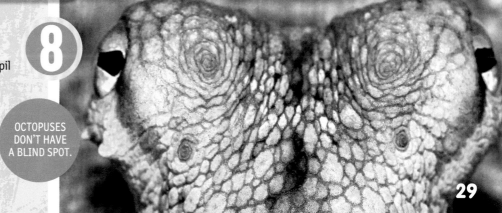

EIGHT Craziest CAVES

DEEP, LONG, ICY, AND HOT—THESE EXTREME CAVES ARE INTENSE THE MOMENT YOU STEP INTO THEM.

① COLD AS ICE

Eisriesenwelt, the largest of Earth's ice caves, stretches for a marathon-like 26 miles (42 km). Hundreds of thousands of tourists visit this fantastic phenomenon—about 37 miles (60 km) south of Salzburg, Austria—every year. If you go, bring a jacket! Temperatures are generally below freezing, even during the summer.

PLENTY OF ELBOW ROOM

2

Vietnam's **Son Doong Cave,** which translates as "Mountain River Cave," isn't the deepest cave or the longest, but it is the widest. How wide, you ask? A passenger plane could comfortably fit inside of it! The cave was discovered in 1990 by a farmer who was seeking cover from a storm.

GRAND AND GLOOMY

3

Mammoth Cave, located in Kentucky, U.S.A., is the world's longest known cave system, with more than 400 miles (644 km) explored. With its stalagmites and stalactites (mineral formations) and its huge chambers, an early guide of the cave once described it as "grand, gloomy, and peculiar." But more than anything else, it's just big!

ALL AGLOW

5

What looks like the setting for a fairy-tale movie is the real-life **Waitomo Glowworm Caves,** a group of 200 caves located in New Zealand. What gives the caves their sparkle? Bioluminescent glowworms, which hang from the ceilings of the cave and twinkle like the night sky.

STEPPING UP

4

The site of a Hindu temple and shrine, **Batu Caves** in Malaysia is a popular destination for both worshippers and tourists. Nestled into limestone cliffs near Kuala Lumpur, the capital city, the site requires visitors to climb several hundred steps to reach the three main caves and numerous smaller ones.

TO THE BAT CAVE!

6

In New Mexico, U.S.A., the **Carlsbad Caverns National Park** is home to more than 100 caves of all sizes. Tourists flock here, but the permanent inhabitants are bats. Every evening during the summer, hundreds of thousands of Brazilian free-tailed bats exit Carlsbad Cavern in a flurry to fly in search of food.

WAY DOWN UNDER

8

To explore Australia's **Olwolgin Cave,** you first have to pull on a scuba mask. In this section of the cave system, a diver weaves through root formations in an area known as the Hanging Gardens of Babylon.

TURN THE PAGE TO VISIT MORE FANTASTIC FORMATIONS!

FUTURE RECORD HOLDER?

7

Uzbekistan's **Dark Star** cave isn't the world's deepest cave (that title belongs to Georgia's Krubera Cave), but it might one day be. Cavers are just getting to know this remote cave system, but the more they explore, the more they are discovering it goes deeper and deeper—and even includes an underground waterfall series.

A-MAZING MAZES

FROM MYTHICAL BEASTS TO STATELY BURIAL CHAMBERS, MAZES HAVE HAD A WINDING HISTORY.

EIGHT MARVELOUS MAZES

① Hampton Court Palace
The intricate, leafy pattern of the maze at England's Hampton Court Palace, built for King William III around 1700, confuses visitors with twists and dead ends. Most people take about 20 minutes to reach the maze's center.

② Corn Maze
Spring Grove, Illinois, U.S.A., farmer Robert Richardson changes the theme of his 33-acre (13-ha) field every year, but the fun stays the same. Grab a flashlight: This one is open late, so you can navigate under the stars.

③ Villa Pisani
This maze in Stra, Italy, highlights the sculptured form of fine garden mazes. With hedges too tall to see over, it's said that Napoleon himself got lost in it.

④ Ice Maze
It took 60,000 ice cubes to create a gigantic maze in Zakopane, Poland, which covered more than half an acre (2,500 sq m).

Mazes and labyrinths have been amusing (and befuddling) humans for thousands of years. Traditionally, labyrinths are designed to lead travelers down a single path, and have no branching subsections to confuse guests. Mazes, on the other hand, are designed with branching sections and dead ends—they are meant to be a puzzle. Today, however, the words are often used interchangeably.

The earliest references to these twisting structures come from the ancient Greeks and Egyptians. In Greek mythology, a terrible beast known as the Minotaur (a half-man, half-bull hybrid) struck fear in the people of Knossos, on the island of Crete in the Mediterranean Sea. So, the king of Knossos asked a man named Daedalus to design a trap that could contain the beast. The maze Daedalus created was so challenging that even he was barely able to make it back out. And when he did, the king imprisoned him and his son, Icarus, to prevent them from telling the maze's secrets. (They escaped by crafting wings out of bird feathers and wax, but Icarus flew too close to the sun, causing his wings to melt.) Could such a fantastical story have some truth in it? Definitely.

A 20th-century archaeologist found the remnants of a labyrinth on Crete, and frescoes on its walls showed the sport of bull jumping, in which a man would jump onto a bull and grab its horns, almost as if they were becoming one creature.

In Egypt, the pyramid complex of King Amenemhet III (ca. 1860-1815 B.C.) was an ancient wonder. As an elaborate series of courts and passageways, the complex was so stunning that the Greek historian Herodotus described it as rivaling the great pyramids of Giza. The king's burial chamber was located at the heart of this maze, protected by false doors and crisscrossing paths. Over the centuries, however, the maze fell into decay, and its materials were even used to build a small town. Nothing is left today except the crumbling remnants of Amenemhet III's pyramid.

Mazes have stuck around from these early traditions. Maze designs can be found on Native American woven baskets, rock carvings in India, and on the floors of Gothic cathedrals. Today, elaborate mazes cut into corn fields or made out of ice blocks provide seasonal entertainment. From stately garden mazes to simple paths that inspire self-reflection, mazes are simply a-mazing.

5 Indoor Maze
In the summer of 2014, the National Building Museum, in Washington, D.C., delighted visitors with a huge maze in its Great Hall. Designed by Danish architect Bjarke Ingels, the maze's outer walls were 18 feet (5.5 m) tall but the inner space shrank to just 3.5 feet (1 m).

6 Van Gogh Maze
In 2015, a maze featuring 125,000 sunflowers was created to celebrate the opening of a new entrance hall to the Van Gogh Museum in Amsterdam, the Netherlands.

7 Patriotic Maze
In 2002, Glen Fritzler designed a 14-acre (5.7-ha) maze in the shape of a bald eagle near LaSalle, Colorado, U.S.A. It had 85 twists and turns along two miles (3.2 km) of paths.

8 Mighty Maze
This French maze in Reignac-sur-Indre returns every year. The elaborate circular pattern of either sunflowers or corn spreads out over 10 acres (4 ha). While the maze looks magical from the air, the real fun is getting lost within its passageways.

FESTIVE PARADES TO GET YOU MARCHING

DO YOU LIKE WATCHING ENORMOUS CHARACTER BALLOONS, PROFESSIONAL DANCERS, OR JUST PLAIN WACKY COSTUMES? THERE'S A PARADE OUT THERE FOR YOU!

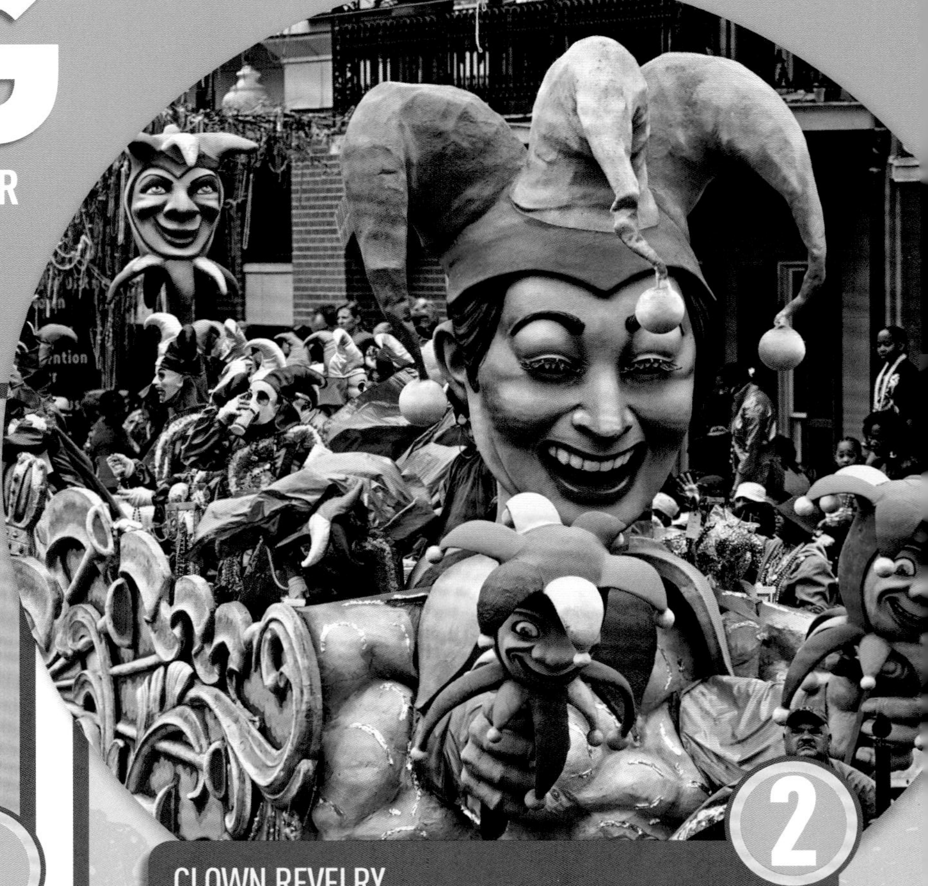

2

CLOWN REVELRY

Giant jester figures parade through the streets of the French Quarter in New Orleans, Louisiana, U.S.A. During the annual **Mardi Gras** celebration, nearly one hundred krewes—or festive groups—toss goodies to the throngs of crowds, including toys, stuffed animals, and plastic Mardi Gras beads.

1

FLOWER POWER

This fantastic float makes its way down the parade route of the 2012 **Rose Parade** on New Year's Day. For more than a century, spectacular flower-covered floats and marching bands have dazzled the crowd at this annual celebration, as does the college football semifinal game that follows the parade.

5

COLORFUL RITUAL

A procession takes place in Nasik, India, during **Kumbh Mela**, a religious pilgrimage undertaken by people of the Hindu faith. The Godavari River, which flows through Nasik, is one of the sites where it's believed that Lord Vishnu dropped sacred nectar during his journey to heaven.

4

VENICE IS SLOWLY SINKING FROM BOTH RISING SEA LEVELS AND DROPPING LAND.

FLOATING FESTIVAL

People in Venice, Italy, take their parades to the water since the Italian city, which is built in a lagoon, has canals for streets. Revelers, including this giant mouse, parade along the Grand Canal in gondolas and other boats during the annual **carnival festival**.

8

NIGHT LIGHTS

Boca Ciega Bay in St. Petersburg, Florida, U.S.A., comes alive with lighted boats during a floating celebration for the Christmas holidays. Participants in the annual St. Pete Beach holiday **boat parade** also donate toys to less fortunate kids. Nice!

7

RIO SAMBA

With elaborate headdresses and costumes, dancers from the Vila Isabel samba school perform in front of the crowd during the 2015 **carnival parade** in Rio de Janeiro, Brazil. The first schools of samba, an Afro-Brazilian dance, were founded in the 1920s.

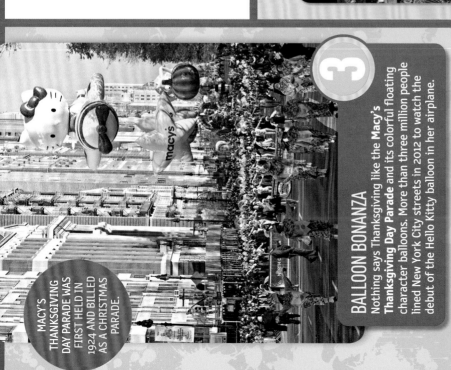

MACY'S THANKSGIVING DAY PARADE WAS FIRST HELD IN 1924 AND BILLED AS A CHRISTMAS PARADE.

3

BALLOON BONANZA

Nothing says Thanksgiving like the **Macy's Thanksgiving Day Parade** and its colorful floating character balloons. More than three million people lined New York City streets in 2012 to watch the debut of the Hello Kitty balloon in her airplane.

BLAZING BOAT

The **Up Helly Aa** festival in Lerwick, Scotland, ends every January with a bang! Harking back to a Viking ritual, a 30-foot (9.2-m)-long galley (longship) goes up in flames after hundreds of torchbearers march through the town's streets to set it on fire.

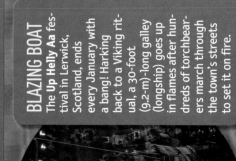

6

1

SYNCHRONIZED SOCCER

Talk about trying to get a leg up on your opponent! Players from Leeds United (left) and Sutton United create a **four-legged soccer** sensation as they battle for the ball during a match in London, England, in early 2017. Sutton United came out on top.

SOCCER BALLS WERE FIRST MADE FROM PIGS' BLADDERS.

EIGHT
WACKIEST SPORTS SHOTS

THESE MIND-TWISTING PHOTOS PROVE THAT THE WIDE WORLD OF SPORTS IS CRAZY INDEED.

2

LEAPING LADY

Marestella Torres of the Philippines appears to fly as she stretches out during the women's **long jump** at the 2009 Asian Athletics Championships in Guangzhou, China. Torres jumped 21.4 feet (6.51 m) to win her nation's first gold medal in the championship.

3

POLE POSITION

How long do I have to hold on? Keisa Monterola from Venezuela shows perfect form during the women's **pole vault** at the 2006 Central American and Caribbean games in Cartagena, Colombia. She won the bronze medal.

UP IN THE AIR

Something gets between Darius Vassell of England and the ball during this soccer match: his airborne opponent, Jorge Andrade of Portugal! Andrade wound up being the high scorer in the end, too. His team won this UEFA Euro 2004 **soccer match.**

4

TURNING HEADS

Look, Ma, no hands—and no head! These Italian figure skaters seem to defy human biology during a 2006 **free dance competition** in Paris. The competitors gathered their body parts to accept the bronze medal in ice dancing at the tournament.

5

6

MIND GAMES

I think I can! Zhu Yuling of China appears to levitate a **table tennis ball** during the final match of a 2016 tournament in Doha, Qatar. The mind trick must have worked: Zhu won the women's title.

7

BASKETBALL BALLET

Say what? The referee seems caught off guard by college basketball player Bashir Ahmed's **big leap,** as he appears to balance the ball on his fingertips in this acrobatic move. Ahmed was actually saving the ball from going out of bounds.

THE FIRST BASKETBALL HOOP WAS MADE FROM A PEACH BASKET.

8

TOE JAM

Who says my feet smell bad?! During this **Tae Kwon Do match,** the players get up close and personal with each other's tootsies. A Korean martial art, Tae Kwon Do is practiced in more than 200 countries.

EIGHT WILDEST CATS

CHECK OUT THE PURR-FECT WAYS THESE LESSER-KNOWN WILD CATS THRIVE IN THEIR DESERT, RAIN FOREST, AND WETLANDS ENVIRONMENTS.

CASTING ABOUT 2

This wild cat earns its name from how it catches its food. With partially webbed feet and double-coated fur to keep it dry, the **fishing cat** plunges into the wetlands where it lives to catch—you guessed it—fish for dinner.

THE CAT'S LONG CLAWS DOUBLE AS FISHING HOOKS.

MAJOR LEAPER 1

At less than two feet (0.6 m) tall, the **caracal** can really catch some air! The reddish brown wild cat has been known to jump over fences more than four times its height to prey on sheep.

NIGHT HIKER 3

Talk about a long-distance traveler. The **black-footed cat** can walk nearly 20 miles (32 km) a night in search of its food. This nocturnal hunter is Africa's smallest wild cat and a versatile eater, with more than 50 species in its diet, including reptiles, insects, and small mammals.

BEARDED BEAUTY
Populations of the endangered **Iberian lynx** suffered a major decline when its main prey, European rabbits, were decimated by disease. But now breeding centers are raising and releasing the scrappy, bearded predators into parts of Spain and Portugal.

4

5

DESERT DWELLER
As one of the smallest wild cats, the **nocturnal sand cat** weighs only around six pounds (2.7 kg). Black fur covers this feline's foot pads and helps protect it from the extreme temperatures in the rocky deserts and sand dunes it calls home.

THE PALLAS'S CAT USES ITS FLUFFY TAIL AS A SCARF TO KEEP IT WARM.

7

ADAPTIVE HUNTER
There's a lot of competition for food in the forests of Mexico and Central and South America where this versatile predator lives. To avoid overlap with other meat-eaters, **jaguarundis** hunt during the day and prey on animals such as rabbits, armadillos, and insects that live on the ground.

6

GRUMPY GUS
Don't be fooled by the disgruntled expression of the **Pallas's cat.** The mysterious wild cat has a reason to smile: It's an Internet sensation in part for the adorable way it hops around, moving low to the ground on the steppes and mountains of its Central Asia habitat.

8

SUPERSIZE TAIL
The **marbled cat's** tail can be as long as its entire body! The feline probably uses its long tail for balance as it hunts in the tropical forests of Southeast Asia. So little is known about this elusive animal that researchers are not even sure what it eats in the wild.

1

BALL OF MIRRORS

Mirrors line the interior of this dazzling dome, a 11.5-foot (3.5-m)-tall hollow hemisphere by Ivana Kuzmonovska and Rachel Couper. **"Mirador"** was formed in part by lasers that cut different-shaped pieces to the designers' specific patterns.

EIGHT

FAR-OUT SCULPTURES **BY THE SEA**

EVERY SPRING FOR TWO DECADES, SURPRISING SCULPTURES HAVE GREETED OCEANGOING VISITORS AT THIS OUTDOOR ART WALK IN SYDNEY, AUSTRALIA.

2

TIME TO GET WET

These works of art really made a splash! In 2015, seven gigantic **spray bottles** offered visitors a way to keep cool. Hooked up to pipes under the sand, the bottles—created by the RCM artist collective—sprayed and dribbled out relief to beach visitors on hot days.

THIS IS NOT A DRILL

During the 2011 exhibition, a young boy creates his own ride out of a **super-size screw** by Danish artist Poul Bækhøj. Sculpture by the Sea is the largest annual sculpture exhibition in the world, hosting approximately half a million visitors and featuring more than 100 sculptures annually by artists worldwide.

4

AMAZING MIRRORS

Mirror, mirror, on the ... sand? With 16 towers shooting up from the sand to reflect both the sun and the passersby, industrial designer Alex Ritchie's **"Kaleidoscope Cube"** offered visitors a new take on their surroundings every time they looked at it.

3

LAND HO!

A giant **breaching whale,** created out of wood by artist Michael Greve, greeted visitors in 2014. As part of the Australian artist's "Sealife Series," the whale captures the fluid movement from sea to sky.

5

GHOST IN THE SHELLS

This translucent sculpture of a young girl by Alessandra Rossi from the 2016 exhibition has an environmental message. **"Untitled Coral"** changes color to show what happens when corals become bleached by expelling their symbiotic algae and turning white.

7

THE ARTIST CREATED THIS SCULPTURE USING A 3-D PRINTER AND TRANSLUCENT ACRYLIC.

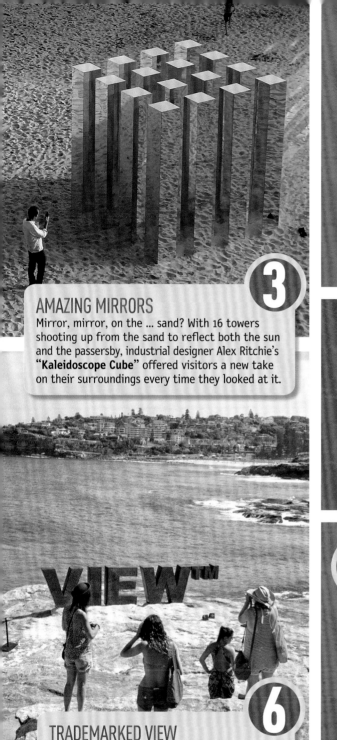

TRADEMARKED VIEW

A sign with a **"view,"** this sculpture exhibited in 2012 suggests that the artist is trying to trademark the scene. While people can trademark logos and brand names, so far no one has been able to trademark spectacular views!

6

TEACHERS HELD LESSONS IN THE PAN ABOUT SUN SAFETY.

FLASH IN THE PAN

A woman "escapes" from a 79-foot (24-m)-wide whimsical **frying pan.** The work, titled "We're Fryin' Out Here," was created to highlight the importance of protecting yourself from skin cancer and not "cooking" yourself on a sun-drenched beach.

8

EIGHT COOL STORIES OF KIDS ON A MISSION

AGE WAS ONLY A NUMBER FOR THESE YOUNG PIONEERS, ADVENTURERS, AND EXPLORERS.

OLD WAGON WHEEL RUTS CAN STILL BE SEEN TODAY ALONG THE OREGON TRAIL.

AT AGE 14, SHIRAISHI CLIMBED A BOULDER RATED AT THE WORLD'S HIGHEST LEVEL FOR DIFFICULTY, BECOMING THE FIRST WOMAN— AND THE YOUNGEST PERSON—TO DO SO.

2 WAGON TRAIN
Let's go West! A family crosses the Great Plains in a covered wagon on the **Oregon Trail.** Some kids in the mid-19th century journeyed nearly 2,000 miles (3,200 km) over four tiring months to reach Oregon or California—and a whole new life.

1 ROCK ON
As a teenager, **Ashima Shiraishi** has set rock-climbing records that adults only dream about. Shiraishi, seen here in 2008 climbing in Central Park in her hometown of New York City, excels at bouldering, or scaling 20-foot (2-m)-tall rocks without ropes or harnesses.

3 RECORD-BREAKER
In 2014, 16-year-old **Lewis Clarke** became the youngest person to ski to the South Pole from the Antarctic coast, with a journey of 702 miles (1,130 km). With winds gusting at 120 miles an hour (193 km/h) and below-freezing temperatures, his Antarctic adventure lasted for almost 50 days.

RUSSIA PLANTED A TITANIUM FLAG ON THE SEABED AT THE NORTH POLE.

5 DRUM BEAT

Children as young as 14 served in the American Civil War (1861–1865). This **drummer boy** would have played different drumrolls to convey the orders from the officers, such as "retreat" and "attack," to the soldiers in battle.

4 POLAR PUSH

In April 2016, at age 14, Australian adventurer **Jade Hameister** became the youngest person to ski to the North Pole—all without the help of any reindeer! Hameister dragged a heavy sled for 93 miles (150 km) on this epic trek.

6 DYNAMIC DUO

Like father, like daughter. In late 2011, the British team of **Amelia Hempleman-Adams** and her explorer father, David Hempleman-Adams, braved Antarctica's deep freeze for 17 nights to ski 97 miles (156 km) to the South Pole. At 16, Amelia became the youngest person at the time to achieve this feat.

7 MAIDEN VOYAGE

In May 2010, 16-year-old Australian teenager **Jessica Watson** arrived in Sydney Harbor, Australia, at the end of her record-setting, 210-day journey to sail around the world by herself unassisted. She navigated more than 23,000 nautical miles (42,600 km) in a 34-foot (10-m) yacht.

8 SURF'S UP

Kyllian Guerin started shredding the waves when he was four years old. The teenage pro-surfer divides his time between France and Costa Rica when he isn't traveling the world and seeking out the best barrels the oceans have to offer.

ROYAL RESIDENCE

This 3-D-printed creation is fit for a prince—or a princess. Andrey Rudenko built this **cement castle** in his own Minnesota, U.S.A., backyard, but first he had to tailor the nozzle on a 3-D printer that usually worked with plastic to use cement instead.

EIGHT

Eye-Popping 3-D-Printed
CREATIONS

CALLING ALL CREATORS! 3-D PRINTING GIVES DESIGNERS THE FREEDOM TO PRINT EVERYTHING FROM TINY TOYS TO HUMONGOUS HOUSES.

THE FIRST 3-D-PRINTED STRATI HAD A GOLF CART MOTOR.

②

ECO-CHIC CAR

The two-seater **Strati,** the world's first 3-D-printed car, is not only for the space age, it's also eco-friendly. Printed in Detroit, Michigan, U.S.A., with the help of the Oak Ridge National Laboratory, the electric car was made from carbon-fire-reinforced plastic and is 100 percent recyclable.

UNIQUE SHOES

④

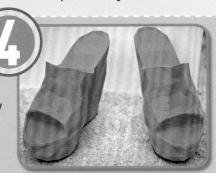

The geometric folds in these orange, 3-D-printed **shoes** are crystal sharp. Style and function join forces with this new technology as artists and designers can realize unique designs and create custom shoes designed for the perfect fit.

③

PENNY PINCHER

This cute **piggy bank** was made at the offices of MakerBot in New York City. The company has more than 460 stores across the United States that sell home 3-D printers and help introduce their customers to the possibilities of 3-D printing.

⑤

HOME SWEET HOME

This two-story **concrete house** was printed in one piece in a neighborhood in Beijing, China. At 4,305 square feet (400 sq m), this home is about the size of a U.S. high school basketball court.

THE HOUSE CAN WITHSTAND A MAGNITUDE 8 EARTHQUAKE.

NANO NANO

Artist Jonty Hurwitz likes things small ... very small. He printed a human form so small she is dwarfed by the **eye of a needle** and impossible to see without a powerful microscope. At 80 x 100 x 20 microns, she fits on a strand of human hair.

⑥

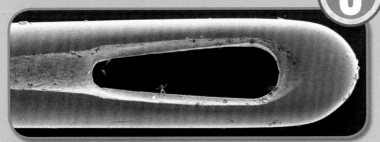

⑧

ROCK ON

At this 2014 design awards ceremony, the Secret Jazz Band from Los Angeles entertained the crowd by playing on a 3-D-printed **guitar and drums.** Rocking out on this red, 3-D-printed instrument shows off how this new technology can carry its own tune.

⑦

FANTASTIC FLIER

It's a bird, it's a plane, it's a 3-D-printed drone called **Thor**! Created by the large airplane manufacturer Airbus, Thor is 13 feet (4 m) long and weighs 46 pounds (21 kg). The only part that's not printed? Its electrical system.

TURN THE PAGE FOR MORE ON 3-D PRINTING!

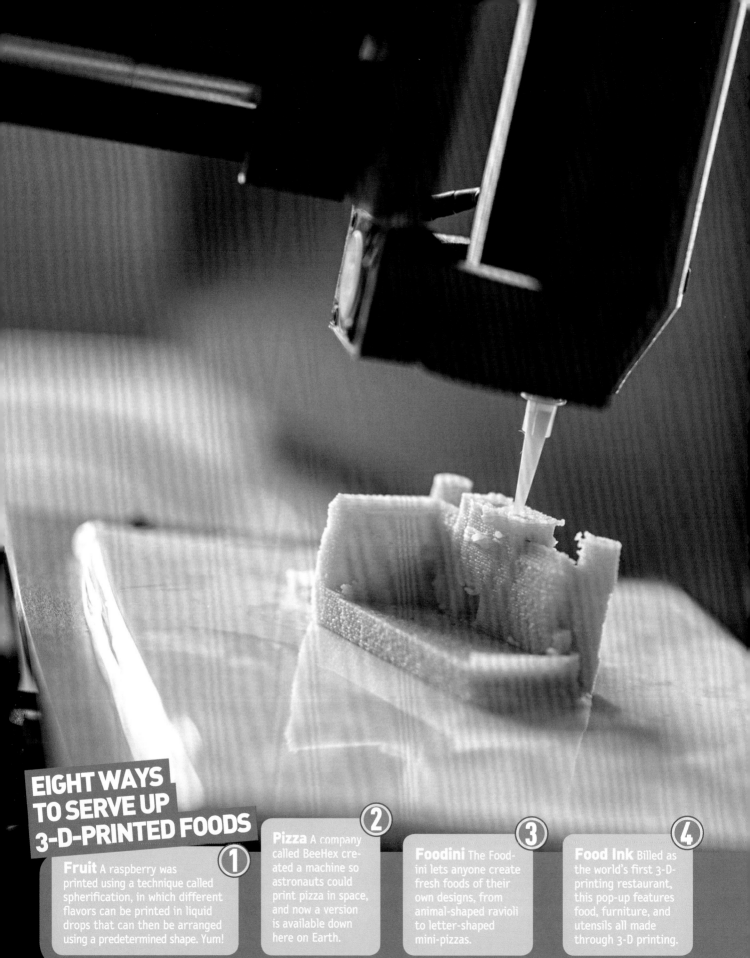

EIGHT WAYS TO SERVE UP 3-D-PRINTED FOODS

① **Fruit** A raspberry was printed using a technique called spherification, in which different flavors can be printed in liquid drops that can then be arranged using a predetermined shape. Yum!

② **Pizza** A company called BeeHex created a machine so astronauts could print pizza in space, and now a version is available down here on Earth.

③ **Foodini** The Foodini lets anyone create fresh foods of their own designs, from animal-shaped ravioli to letter-shaped mini-pizzas.

④ **Food Ink** Billed as the world's first 3-D-printing restaurant, this pop-up features food, furniture, and utensils all made through 3-D printing.

HOW DOES 3-D PRINTING WORK?

IT'S CHANGING EVERYTHING FROM ENVIRONMENTALLY FRIENDLY CARS TO BODY PARTS.

Every day, some amazing new object is made using 3-D printing. But what is this technology anyway? And how does it work?

Instead of printing on a flat piece of paper, like an inkjet printer does, a 3-D printer forms objects by layering materials in a specific pattern. The pattern comes from a blueprint that tells the printer how to build the item, layer by layer.

What can these printers make? Many home 3-D printers (yes, people have them at home—but they're pretty expensive!) use plastic that is heated to melt and then is extruded (forced out) through a nozzle. As the layers add up, they cool and harden. But plastic isn't the only material used by these devices. Scientists, engineers, and designers experiment with metals like silver, steel, and titanium, wax or cement—and even food like pasta, chocolate, and pizza (see sidebar).

The technology seems far-out. That's partly what makes it so exciting ... and useful. When humans journey to Mars, there likely will be mishaps. With a 3-D printer, designs of replacement parts can be sent directly to the red planet and then printed to form the needed parts. That provides an important safety net for wannabe Martians.

But 3-D printing is also working some wonders on Earth. When a six-year-old bald eagle was found with a damaged top beak—emaciated and unable to eat—an animal wildlife rehabilitator named Jane Fink Cantwell was able to nurse her back to health. But Cantwell also wanted to give the majestic bird, called Beauty, a chance at a normal life.

That's where a team of engineers and animal experts, including a dentist, came in. They crafted and fit a 3-D version of the missing part of the beak during a two-hour surgery. This gave Beauty her beak—and her groove!—back.

And when Jake Evill broke his arm, it had to be set in a plaster cast. Bummer! But the graduate of New Zealand's University of Wellington wasn't just irritated; he was motivated! He designed a latticework 3-D-printed cast that allowed his skin to breathe. Called Cortex, the washable and recyclable cast, only .12 inch (3 mm) thick, is also super lightweight.

From helping wildlife on Earth to assisting astronauts on space missions, 3-D printing is revolutionizing our world. The possibilities are virtually limitless.

5 Farming Some farmers in Myanmar are using 3-D-printed parts for their equipment to increase efficiency.

6 Castle A 3-D printer built an edible model of the 19th-century Neuschwanstein Castle, a romantic fortress in Bavaria, Germany.

7 Candy The Magic Candy Factory in Birmingham, United Kingdom, offers giant gummy candies in all kinds of shapes, from cars to castles to crabs!

8 Breakfast A 3-D printer called PancakeBot can print pancakes by dropping batter directly onto a griddle. And users can create their own fun designs!

Unconventional
ACCOMMODATIONS

ATTENTION TRAVELERS: THESE COZY, CURIOUS, AND COMPLETELY ODD HOTELS ADD ADVENTURE IN EVERY ROOM.

1 ATMOSPHERIC MAGIC

Travelers at this hotel in Levi, Finland, can drift off to sleep while watching the spellbinding colors of the northern lights through **glass-ceiling igloos.** Auroras can only be seen in locations near the poles, so this location above the Arctic Circle is in a picture-perfect spot!

DURING THE WINTER, TEMPERATURES IN LEVI CAN REMAIN BELOW ZERO AND EVEN DIP TO MINUS 58°F (-50°C),

2 JURASSIC HOTEL

The front desk of this hotel in Tokyo, Japan, is dino-mite! At the **Henn-na (Weird) Hotel,** a multilingual raptor robot checks guests into their rooms. The hotel is also within walking distance of Tokyo Disneyland. Positively prehistoric!

5 CAVE WITH A VIEW

At night this **cave hotel** in Cappadocia, Turkey, really sparkles. The region's mesmerizing landscape formed after an eruption about three million years ago blanketed the region with volcanic ash. Wind and rain then carved shapes into the soft rock.

8 CHOO-CHOO

Just 100 feet (30 m) from the Indian Ocean, every room at the Santos Express **train hotel** in Mossel Bay, South Africa, has a view of the waves. The hotel's bunks are in refurbished train cars, and with whale-watching and shark-cage-diving close by, the adventure doesn't stop at the shoreline.

4 LIVING IN A BUBBLE

On a clear night you can see, well, everything! This **transparent abode** in the woods of the south of France is not for the shy at heart. But if you want to be able to sleep under the stars without bugs bursting your bubble, this may be your jam.

7 SEA AND SUN

This three-story **underwater room** on Pemba Island, Tanzania, will really float your boat! There is an upper deck for sunbathing or stargazing, a bathroom and lounge at sea level, and a lower level for watching shoals of fish and sea life swim past—from the comfort of your bed.

3 BOOK BUNKS

With 3,200 books to choose from at this **"capsule" hotel** in Tokyo, Japan, there's no excuse not to read before bed. Guests stay in two types of micro-rooms: ones located in nooks behind the bookshelves or in bunks. This hotel gives new meaning to "booking" your accommodations!

6 MODERN MASTERPIECE

Hotel or modern artwork? This **luxury hotel** in Elciego, Spain, is both. Designed by world-famous architect Frank Gehry, the building itself is a visionary landmark. The colors of the titanium façade represent the region's tradition of fine wine.

49

SEA TURTLES AREN'T BOTHERED BY BOX JELLYFISH'S VENOM AND ARE ONE OF THE FEW ANIMALS THAT EAT THEM.

1 NO STRINGS ATTACHED

A **box jellyfish** wields its powerful toxins for self-protection. The nearly invisible invertebrates use their venom, which is found in cells in their tentacles and is considered to be one of the deadliest in the world, to stun prey—fish and shrimp—so they don't wriggle, get tangled, and cause damage to the jellyfish's tentacles.

EIGHT

FREAKIEST ANIMAL EXTREMES

THERE'S NOTHING ORDINARY ABOUT THESE CREATURES: BIG, OTHERWORLDLY, POISONOUS, EVEN HUNGRY FOR BLOOD—THEY EACH EXEMPLIFY AN EPIC ANIMAL ODDITY!

2 THIS IS NO FAIRY TALE

About five inches (13 cm) long, the rarely seen, underground-dwelling **pink fairy armadillo** has a light-pink armored shell that functions kind of like a radiator. The compact critter can actually raise or lower its core temperature by pumping blood in and out of its shell. Extremely cool!

THE INDIGENOUS EMBERÁ PEOPLE OF COLOMBIA USE THE FROG'S VENOM IN THEIR BLOW DARTS FOR HUNTING.

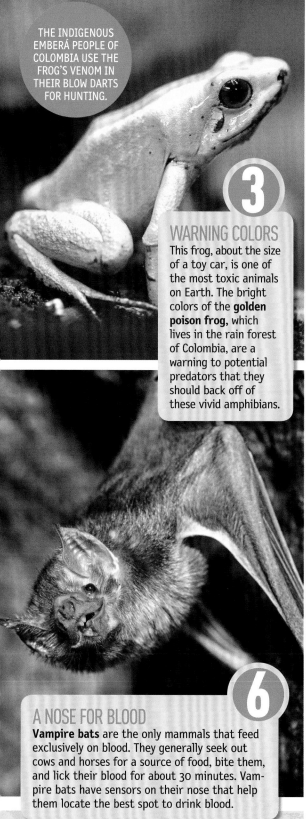

3 WARNING COLORS

This frog, about the size of a toy car, is one of the most toxic animals on Earth. The bright colors of the **golden poison frog**, which lives in the rain forest of Colombia, are a warning to potential predators that they should back off of these vivid amphibians.

4 HIDDEN WEAPON

Male **platypuses** have a trick up their sleeve—or rather, up their feet. They have spurs on the heels of their hind feet, which they use to deliver a toxic blow to enemies. Scientists have discovered that the poison contains a hormone that could one day help treat diabetes in humans.

HOLY MOLA! 5

Weighing up to 5,000 pounds (2,250 kg), the sunfish, also known as a **mola**, is the world's heaviest bony fish. But it still looks like only half a fish, because the back fin that it is born with never grows! Its extremely unusual shape makes it an awkward swimmer; it's often seen cruising the ocean's surface, basking in the sun.

OUTSIZE INSECTS

Asian giant hornets are—you guessed it!—pretty big, measuring two inches (5 cm) long with a wingspan of three inches (8 cm). They can sting a person through a rain jacket and under extreme circumstances, can be deadly to humans and honeybees. As the world's largest hornets, they are helpful in keeping crop-munching caterpillars in check.

6 A NOSE FOR BLOOD

Vampire bats are the only mammals that feed exclusively on blood. They generally seek out cows and horses for a source of food, bite them, and lick their blood for about 30 minutes. Vampire bats have sensors on their nose that help them locate the best spot to drink blood.

THAT'S A BIG BUG

The world's heaviest insect—**the giant weta**—weighs as much as a blue jay. Though big, this native New Zealand member of the cricket family is not dangerous. It hides in dead foliage during the day and comes out at night to feast on plants.

8

PURPLE POWER

The striking purple **amethyst** gemstone was pricey like emeralds and rubies until the 1800s, when massive deposits were found in Brazil. After that, the purple quartz mineral that had been coveted by royalty for hundreds of years became affordable for the masses.

ONE SINGLE AMETHYST CRYSTAL WEIGHED 164 POUNDS (74 KG).

EIGHT
RADDEST ROCKS AND MINERALS

MOTHER NATURE IS A MASTER ARTIST, ESPECIALLY WHEN IT COMES TO PRECIOUS GEMS AND STRIKING STONES.

SOME GEODES ARE SO LARGE YOU CAN STAND INSIDE OF THEM.

INNER BEAUTY

Geodes are spherical rocks that form in a variety of ways, from bubbles in volcanic rock to mud balls formed on the bottoms of rivers and other water bodies. Over millions of years, the shell hardens and crystals form inside, creating an artistic, almost magical interior of patterns and colors.

FOOL'S GOLD

4

This is one tricky stone. **Pyrite** can mirror the appearance of real gold, but it's brittle and leaves brownish streaks, whereas gold is supple and leaves yellow streaks. Fool's gold does have one shining asset: It sparks when struck against a rock.

SEE-THROUGH PRISMS

3

Colorless or with a whitish hue, the translucent crystal **scolecite** mimics city skyscrapers radiating upward and outward from a central point. First discovered in Iceland, the gem takes its name from the Greek word for "worm" because of how it curls up when heated.

BLUE BEAUTY

5

The deep blue crystals of this mineral form of **calcium fluoride** (that's right, the stuff you may find in toothpaste) are gorgeous. But it also has a more far-out use—it's used to make telescope lenses.

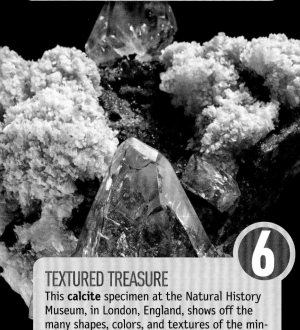

RAINBOW ROCK

7

A thin layer of titanium coats this **quartz crystal** to give it sparkling, iridescent colors. The process takes place in a vacuum chamber where the natural electrical charge of the crystal bonds with the titanium to create a stunning sparkle.

TEXTURED TREASURE

6

This **calcite** specimen at the Natural History Museum, in London, England, shows off the many shapes, colors, and textures of the mineral made of calcium carbonate. Also made of calcium carbonate? The pearls your mom or grandma may wear on special occasions.

RARE GEM

8

Is it a sparkling sea creature? An unusual plant? Nope. These slender shards make up a sample of **carminite**, a rare gem formed in rock deposits containing lead. The small, delicate crystals of this mineral form elaborate designs that make you do a double take.

EIGHT
MIND-BLOWING
ILLUSIONS

REAL LIFE LOOKS LIKE SCIENCE FICTION WHEN YOU CATCH A GLIMPSE AT CLOSE RANGE.

THE LEANING TOWER OF PISA HAD ALREADY STARTED TO LEAN WHEN WORKERS WERE BUILDING THE THIRD STORY.

2

LEAN ON ME

Whoa! You're a little crooked, **Leaning Tower of Pisa!** Forced perspective photos use optical illusions—and good prop placement—to make people or objects seem larger or smaller, like this girl "holding up" the tower.

1

GIVE ME A HAND?

Graphic designer Kyle Huber knows about being at the right place at the right time. In this case, using his free hand to appear to **lift up a "tiny" friend** from a rock. The friend is actually standing in the distance, while Huber uses his other hand to capture the shot with his camera.

3

TRYING TO FIT IN

Made you do a double take? With the right props and the perfect angle, this vehicle doesn't look a bit out of the ordinary—except that it's a **toy car!** By keeping the toy close to the camera's lens, the other cars seem to be the same scale.

BALANCING ACT

What a crack-up! These men, balancing at a salt lake in Bolivia, aren't standing on eggs—they're merely standing on one foot. The photographer perfectly positioned **two eggs** near the camera's lens to create this eggs-quisite effect.

4

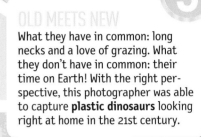

OLD MEETS NEW

What they have in common: long necks and a love of grazing. What they don't have in common: their time on Earth! With the right perspective, this photographer was able to capture **plastic dinosaurs** looking right at home in the 21st century.

5

"TAXI!"

At first glance, this looks like another New Yorker hailing a cab on a rainy day in the city. Except it's actually an action figure named **The Normal Man,** who is carefully positioned and photographed doing "normal" things like working at an office, cooking in his kitchen, and—ahem!—using the toilet.

6

THE NORMAL MAN HAS MORE THAN 60,000 FOLLOWERS ON INSTAGRAM.

7

HUT, HUT, HIKE!

This looks like foul play! A boy **buried in the sand** with just his head showing was the perfect prop for a playful football scene, while his teammate hunkered over perfectly so his own head disappeared. Score!

8

AHOY, THERE!

This artist creates stories by mixing everyday objects with **miniature figurines** in unique settings. In this case, a green shoelace may be a sea serpent to the captain and first mate of this bottle-cap ship.

①

FEET FIRST!

Flying down the ice at more than 80 miles an hour (129 km/h) on a sled that rests on a pair of razor-sharp blades shows a serious need for speed! **Luge** is a winter Olympic sport, but in the off-season there's always street luge—heading down steep, paved streets on a luge with wheels!

— EIGHT

SPEEDIEST SPORTS

THINK FAST! IF YOU BLINK, YOU'LL MISS THE ACTION IN THESE QUICKSILVER SPORTS.

②

FASTER WITH AGE

The game of **cricket** has been around for 800 years or so, but the speed at which the ball is thrown gets faster and faster. In 2003, a cricket ball was bowled at a record speed of 100.23 miles an hour (161.3 km/h)—just a few miles an hour slower than the fastest baseball pitch.

④ NO TIME TO SPARE

Driving at speeds up to 231.5 miles an hour (372.6 km/h), **Formula One** race car drivers can't waste a single second to win a race. When they pull in for a pit stop, a four-tire change takes about two seconds!

BECAUSE RACE CAR COCKPITS ARE SO HOT, DRIVERS LOSE SEVERAL POUNDS EVERY RACE FROM SWEATING!

③ CATCHY STEPS

What's yellow, fuzzy, and travels at 163 miles an hour (262 km/h)? Not a bird. Not a plane. A **tennis ball!** Imagine returning that serve when all you see coming is a yellow blur. The fastest moving tennis balls travel at the same speed as a commercial jet at takeoff!

⑤ FLY BIRDIE

What's faster than a race car? A badminton birdie, of course! The fastest birdie ever hit flew 253.55 miles an hour (408 km/h), making **badminton** the fastest racquet sport. Basic birdies are made of nylon, but Olympians use birdies made from goose feathers.

⑥ FORE!

Here's a reason to stay alert on the links: The fastest recorded **golf** drive was clocked at 217.1 miles an hour (349.38 km/h). Not all golf balls are the same, though. The number of dimples ranges from 400 to 1,000— the more dimples, the farther a ball generally travels.

⑦ A LOT OF BACK AND FORTH

This isn't an ordinary Ping-Pong game. Professional **table tennis** players can hit a ball as fast as 163.4 miles an hour (263 km/h)—that's quicker than the world's fastest roller coaster! Table tennis is an Olympic sport, with elite-level games lasting as long as 30 minutes.

⑧ SLAP SHOT!

There's a reason **ice hockey** goalies wear face masks. Pucks can fly at speeds of more than 100 miles an hour (161 km/h)! To make pucks go even faster, the pucks are frozen before professional hockey games. It makes them glide smoother and prevents bouncing.

EIGHT Stupendous SLIDES

AWESOME ADVENTURES CAN BE FOUND AROUND EVERY TWIST AND TURN OF THESE CHARISMATIC CHUTES.

1 A DROP IN THE OCEAN

A **cruise ship** passenger enjoys a twisting, superfast slide on the lido deck. Cruise ships started to add water slides on board in the 1970s, but those were more like the sleepy slides you'd find in a playground. Today, shipboard slides are designed to thrill. Good thing times have changed!

CHILD'S PLAY

One of the three chutes at this Swedish playground is sure to be the right fit. The slides are part of the amusement park **Astrid Lindgren's World,** which celebrates the world of the children's book author who gave us Pippi Longstocking.

CHILL ZONE

A mother and child experience the thrill of an icy chill while speeding down an **ice slide** at Harbin Ice Wonderland in Bangkok, Thailand. Visitors take a break from the tropical heat outside to experience the ice park, where fun is had at a chilly 5°F (-15°C).

AN ELEPHANT CAN DRINK 10 GALLONS (38 L) OF WATER IN ONE MINUTE.

ARTY TWIST

In 2006, when German artist Carsten Höller installed five **stainless steel slides** in the Tate Modern gallery in London, England, for a six-month exhibit, he added a whole new twist to a contemporary art museum. At 182 feet (55.5 m), the longest chute gave museumgoers an easy way to let off steam.

ELEPHANT ANTICS

This pachyderm's trunk transforms into a **whimsical slide** for a young girl. Real flesh-and-blood elephants can twist and turn their trunks in complex ways by using about 100,000 muscle units.

DARING DROP

This looping monstrosity in Queen Elizabeth Olympic Park in London, England, is a record holder in more ways than one. At 584 feet (178 m), the **ArcelorMittal Orbit** is not only the world's tallest and longest tunnel slide but also the tallest structure in the United Kingdom.

THE SLIDE CONTAINS ENOUGH STEEL TO MAKE 265 DOUBLE-DECKER BUSES.

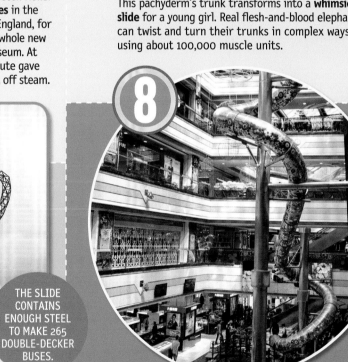

SKY SLIDE

Getting from the 70th to the 69th floor in the U.S. Bank Tower in Los Angeles can be an adrenaline-pumping affair. The 45-foot (14-m) steel-and-glass **Skyslide,** which is attached to the outside of the building, offers 360-degree views of La La Land.

SHOP TILL YOU SLIDE

Shoppers at this **mall** in Shanghai, China, can burn off any excess energy by sliding down five stories. The trip down the 177-foot (54-m)-long twisting structure takes about 16 seconds. Then it's back to shopping!

UNCANNY ANIMALS OF THE GALÁPAGOS

THERE ARE NO OTHER ANIMALS LIKE THEM: THESE CREATURES EXIST ONLY IN AND AROUND THE GALÁPAGOS ISLANDS.

2 LEAPING LOCUSTS!

It's no surprise that **large painted locusts** are related to grasshoppers; both insects share a super jumping ability. The locusts can leap 9.8 feet (3 m), which serves them well when trying to flee their predators: lava lizards and Galápagos hawks.

1 WILLING TO ADAPT

Penguins in warm waters? **Galápagos penguins,** which live farther north than any other penguin on Earth, are the only penguins that inhabit the Northern Hemisphere. And they've found creative ways to adapt to their island habitat: They build nests from lava rocks!

3 A BIRD THAT MOOS

The **waved albatross,** the largest bird on the Galápagos, has a wingspan of 7.2 feet (2.2 m), but what's even more impressive is its courtship dance. Couples nod heads, clack their bills, waddle, and let out a cowlike moo!

GALÁPAGOS TORTOISES HAVE BEEN LIVING ON THE ISLANDS FOR THREE MILLION YEARS.

CATCHING Z'S

5

Like many sea lions, **Galápagos sea lions** can be found on beaches and docks lounging about. They head to the sea to catch fish, but generally stick close to shore. About 50,000 sea lions call the Galápagos home.

OLD-TIMERS

4

Galápagos tortoises are the longest living vertebrates, surviving as many as 152 years! Hunting and the introduction of non-native species have lowered their numbers, and they are now protected by the government. Galápagos tortoises eat grasses, leaves, and cactus and sleep up to 16 hours a day.

WINGS MADE FOR SWIMMING

7

Flightless cormorants have adapted to no longer need their wings for flight; they dive into the water for their food. Living on just two islands in the Galápagos, they do use their wings to help steer them to prey, which includes octopus, fish, and squid.

YOU CALLING ME CLUMSY?

8

English naturalist Charles Darwin called **marine iguanas** the "most disgusting, clumsy lizards." These remote reptiles have a unique adaptation: They are the only iguanas that can swim and forage underwater. Although they look fierce, they survive almost exclusively on algae.

TOP HUNTER

6

One of the only natural predators on the islands, the **Galápagos hawk** feeds on anything it can get its talons on: rodents, birds, lizards, baby tortoises, and sea turtles. It uses the same nest over several seasons that is up to 9.8 feet (3 m) deep!

MARINE IGUANAS SNEEZE FREQUENTLY TO GET RID OF SEA SALT FROM GLANDS NEAR THEIR NOSE.

TURN THE PAGE FOR MORE ON THESE AMAZING ISLANDS!

THE ENCHANTED ISLANDS

THE PLACE OF OTHERWORLDLY ANIMALS HAS INTRIGUED SCIENTISTS FOR ALMOST 200 YEARS.

Six hundred miles (966 km) from the mainland of South America, the Galápagos Islands—first known as Las Encantadas, or, "The Enchanted Ones"—are one of the most isolated places on Earth. Long ago, animals ventured to the islands—by flight, by sea, or by accident. Only those that were able to adapt to the conditions there survived and thrived.

In 1835, a ship named the H.M.S. *Beagle* arrived at the islands with a passenger on board named Charles Darwin. Darwin was a young naturalist, and along with other scientists, he studied specimens that he collected on the Galápagos. Through his observations, he began to form theories about how species adapt by natural selection—those with the traits that are most suitable to an environment survive and produce offspring, passing on those adaptations. For

example, Darwin famously examined the beaks of the same species of birds from different islands of the Galápagos and found that, even though the islands were just a few miles apart, the birds adapted to have beaks that specially suited the kinds of seeds they ate on their particular island.

But it wasn't just birds that adapted. Marine iguanas, which are only found on the Galápagos Islands, diverged from land iguanas some 10 million years ago. To hunt for the algae they need to survive, they evolved to be able to swim underwater, using special claws to grip the rocks. During lean years, marine iguanas have even adapted to get shorter. They absorb their bone and reduce their size by 20 percent to survive on less and then grow again when more food is available!

EIGHT OTHER COOL THINGS IN THE GALÁPAGOS

1 Volcanoes The Galápagos are one of the most volcanically active places on Earth, with more than 50 eruptions in the past 200 years.

2 Marine Reserve Marine life and the waters surrounding the islands are protected by the Galápagos Marine Reserve.

3 Lava Lizards Male lava lizards defend their territory by extending the scales on their back and bobbing up and down.

4 Lava Tunnels On Isla Santa Cruz, underground tunnels were formed when molten lava flows solidified.

Puerto Egas Beach ⑤
The sands on this beach are black thanks to Isla Santiago's volcanic rock.

Sharks ⑥ The waters surrounding the Galápagos hold more sharks than anywhere else on Earth.

Blue-footed Boobies ⑦ They get their name from their colorful feet, which males use in their awkward dance to attract females.

Fog ⑧ The *garúa* is a dense fog that covers the junglelike highlands of the Galápagos.

BIZARRE BUILDINGS

THESE UNIQUE JAW-DROPPING STRUCTURES CAN BE FOUND ALL OVER THE WORLD, FROM SMALL TOWNS TO A DESERT METROPOLIS.

THE BUILDING'S UNIQUE SHAPE MEANS IT HAS THE SAME FLOOR SPACE AS A VERTICAL BUILDING WITH 40 STORIES.

2 ROUND WONDER

There's no bad view from the **headquarters of Aldar,** a real estate company in Abu Dhabi, United Arab Emirates. The 23-floor, spherical building also performs as well as it looks: An underground recycling facility reuses waste from the building.

1 DIAMOND DAZZLER

The diamond-shaped **national library of Belarus,** located in the capital city of Minsk, uses natural light to shine during the day. But at night it performs its own light show, with more than 4,600 LED fixtures that can be controlled for different effects.

3 TRUNK TOWER

The **Chang Building** in Bangkok, Thailand, should be called the Pachyderm Palace. At 335 feet (102 m) high, the elephant-shaped building includes offices, apartments, and even a shopping mall. And this building's "ears" are actually multilevel balconies.

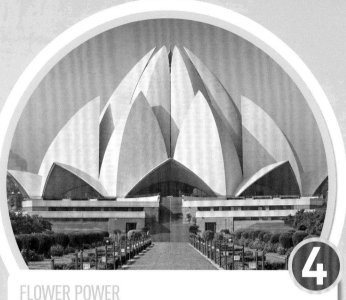

FLOWER POWER

Thousands of people visit the Bahá'í **Lotus Temple** in New Delhi, India, every day. Nine is a mystical number for the followers of the Bahá'í faith, and nine pools surround 27 marble "lotus" petals, which make the temple appear to float on water.

4

5

SHOE STOPPER

The **Haines Shoe House** looks like it was made for hiking, but this boot near York, Pennsylvania, U.S.A., has a sweet side: Passersby can find gourmet ice cream and other treats inside. At nearly three stories tall and 48 feet (15 m) long, this is one boot-iful building.

7

TEA TIME

This 10-story-tall building isn't designed to make an extremely large cup of morning brew. The **Wuxi Wanda Cultural Tourism City Exhibition Center** in Wuxi, China, pays homage to local teapot culture. A mini-roller coaster, Ferris wheel, and movable sand table are located inside.

6

BLAZING BUILDINGS

These towers in Baku, Azerbaijan, are hot! Not only are they the tallest buildings in the capital city, rising some 800 feet (244 m), they also contain living and office spaces. What makes the **Flame Towers** really sizzle? At night, they light up as if they're on fire.

8

FLOWING FACADE

The **Museum of Pop Culture** in Seattle, Washington, U.S.A., changes its look depending on the light and the viewer's location. Three thousand panels made of 21,000 aluminum and steel shingles give the building its fluid form.

ALL THE STEEL USED IN THE BUILDING, STRETCHED OUT TO BE AS LIGHT AS THE THINNEST BANJO STRING, WOULD REACH A QUARTER OF THE WAY TO VENUS.

Eccentric UPCYCLED CREATIONS

ALL OF THESE COMPLETELY CAPTIVATING CREATIONS ARE MADE FROM RECYCLED GOODS.

2 BREAKFAST FASHION

Designer Ami Goodheart created this tasty shirt and **edible pants** for the Hunger Pains fashion series. The top includes banana peels and carrots while the model sports waffles for the pants. Could he have some maple syrup to go with the pants?

1 FLIPPING OUT

Jackson Mbatha looks into the eye of his toy giraffe, a colorful eco-sculpture he created from pieces of discarded **flip-flops.** The company he works for, Ocean Sole in Nairobi, Kenya, cleans up the country's beaches and rivers to find raw material for amazing masterpieces like this one.

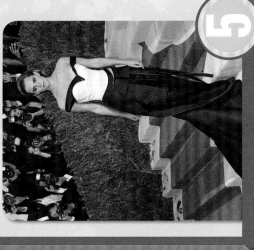

5 STAR POWER

Movie star and UN Women Goodwill Ambassador **Emma Watson** sports a custom Calvin Klein dress made from recycled plastic bottles at a fashion benefit in 2016 for the Metropolitan Museum of Art's Costume Institute in New York City. That's eco-friendly elegance!

8 RUNNING ON PLASTIC

This plastic sneaker, the **Adidas x Parley**, is not just stylish, it's eco-fashionable, because it's made from plastic reclaimed and recycled from the ocean. With more than an estimated eight million tons (7,257,500 t) of plastic clogging the big blue sea, that's a win-win!

4 FORK-TASTIC

A four-pronged fork provided the raw material for this affectionate piece of **jewelry.** By taking goods that would otherwise be thrown out and recycling them into new creations, upcycling is great for the globe and for the imagination.

7 FAN-CY DRESS

The creator of this ensemble turned **junk mail** into the radiating fans on its skirt, which took 200 hours to craft. Canvas scraps and discarded mail such as ads from newspapers and catalogs add an eco-friendly spin to this Spanish-style dress.

3 SUPER SATCHEL

A woman in Nairobi, Kenya, turns **plastic bags,** the ubiquitous by-product of our modern society, into durable, handcrafted bags. The project by Tosheka Textiles supports hundreds of crafty women by giving them a way to earn money and protect the environment.

IT'S ESTIMATED THAT MORE THAN 500 BILLION PLASTIC BAGS ARE USED EACH YEAR GLOBALLY.

6 BEEP BEEP

An attendee at the Los Angeles Auto Show was spotted carrying this **license plate purse.** Metal license plates are often recycled, but with this twist, they get a new life as a one-of-a-kind treasure.

SOMETHING'S FISHY

This heart is sealed with a fish! Humboldt penguins at the ZSL **London Zoo** in England were offered fish frozen in heart-shaped ice blocks in honor of Valentine's Day. Love was in the air: The holiday coincided with the time of year when penguins choose their nest-mates.

EIGHT

ZANIEST ZOO ATTRACTIONS

THESE ANIMALS DON'T GO TO PARTIES—THE PARTIES COME TO THEM! ZOOS AROUND THE WORLD FIND UNIQUE WAYS TO KEEP ANIMALS BUSY AND VISITORS ENTERTAINED.

2

TABLE MANNERS, PLEASE!

Somebody better tell these ring-tailed lemurs at the **San Francisco Zoo** to keep their elbows (and tails) off the table! The group was treated to a Thanksgiving Day feast that included green beans, bananas, sweet potatoes, and a turkey made from kibble.

A GROUP OF LEMURS IS CALLED A TROOP.

MAKE A WISH

Fu Ni, a giant panda living in Australia's **Adelaide Zoo,** got a "cake" to celebrate her fourth birthday. Inside the cardboard cake-shaped box was her real treat—some of her favorite fruits.

BALANCING ACT

Animals at Germany's **Hannover Adventure Zoo** enjoyed an Easter egg hunt tailored just for them: eggs containing their favorite treats! This lucky sea lion, named Pamela, shows off her egg-cellent balancing skills.

COOL SNACK

On a hot day at Israel's **Zoological Center Tel Aviv-Ramat Gan,** a Syrian brown bear gets an icy cold treat: frozen chunks with fruit—and fish!—inside. The Popsicles not only beat the heat, but they also added a good mental challenge for the bear, who had to figure out how to get at the snacks frozen inside.

A COLONY OF MEERKATS SLEEPS IN ONE BIG PILE.

NIGHT LIGHTS

Washington, D.C.'s **National Zoo** comes alive at night during winter's ZooLights, an annual display of more than 500,000 eco-friendly lights, including a light show set to music. Nocturnal animals take center stage at indoor exhibits, where visitors can come in from the cold and thaw their "paws."

TRICK OR TREAT?

This cheeky meerkat at the **Hellabrunn Zoo** in Munich, Germany, found the perfect costume when it crawled inside a jack-o'-lantern. The festive pumpkin was given to him by zookeepers in celebration of Halloween.

CHRISTMAS DOWN UNDER

This wallaby must have been on Santa's nice list! Animals big and small at Sydney, Australia's **Taronga Zoo** got special treats for Christmas, including hanging pinecones decorated with special snacks for the picking, which helps promote their natural curiosity.

EIGHT FOODS TOO ARTISTIC TO EAT

FOOD CAN BE FUN! THESE ARTISTS PUT A NEW TWIST ON SOME FAVORITE TREATS.

HOME SWEET HOME

2

These hand-painted cookies look too good to eat! **Sugar cookies** can be traced back to Nazareth, Pennsylvania, U.S.A., when—in the mid-1700s—German settlers created the round, buttery cookies and the recipe caught on. Eventually, decorated sugar cookies became a holiday tradition.

DANGEROUSLY GOOD

1

Quick! Eat this before it devours you! Brek Nebel, a dad from Washington State, U.S.A., whips up these **fancy pancakes** for his son's breakfast. He says his pancakes take about 45 minutes to make and are often inspired by whatever his son is interested in that day.

GOING BANANAS

3

Artist Jessica Siskin (also known as "Misterkrisp") sculpts Rice Krispies into edible works of art, including cheeseburgers, taxis, emojis, people, and animals like this **hungry little monkey.** Siskin uses food coloring to help bring these clever creations to life.

⑤ NO TRICKS! JUST TREATS!

Now here's a lunch that won't scare you away from cleaning your plate! This creative **bento box** lunch makes a traditional PB&J look like child's play. Bento boxes originated in Japan and typically are divided into sections to separate out types of foods.

IN 17TH-CENTURY JAPAN, PEOPLE TOOK BENTO BOXES TO THE THEATER AND ATE A SNACK FROM THEM AT INTERMISSION.

④ #DELICIOUS!

Scottish photographer Heather Adamson doesn't just send **emojis** to friends via text, she constructs them in her kitchen and posts them on social media. This smiling face with sunglasses was created with pieces of mango and pineapple, and chia seeds.

⑥ HOOT FOR FRUIT

Well, that's one way to carve a watermelon! **Fruit carving** is an art form, especially in Thailand, where sweet treats including melons and apples are canvases waiting to be sculpted. Fruit carving is such an important part of Thai tradition that it is taught as a class in schools.

⑦ DOODLEWICH

Looks like lunch is going to be tied up for a bit! A graphic artist based in Massachusetts, U.S.A., adds designs on his kids' **sandwich bags** every day before packing their lunches. Drawing everything from robots to monsters, he tries to incorporate the shape of the bread into his unusual artwork.

⑧ ROLLING WITH IT

This **sushi sloth,** created by sushi artist Tama-chan, is an edible work of art. Using ingredients found in traditional sushi, Tama-chan pays attention to details, including making a hole in the center so this sloth has something to hold onto—a chopstick, perhaps?

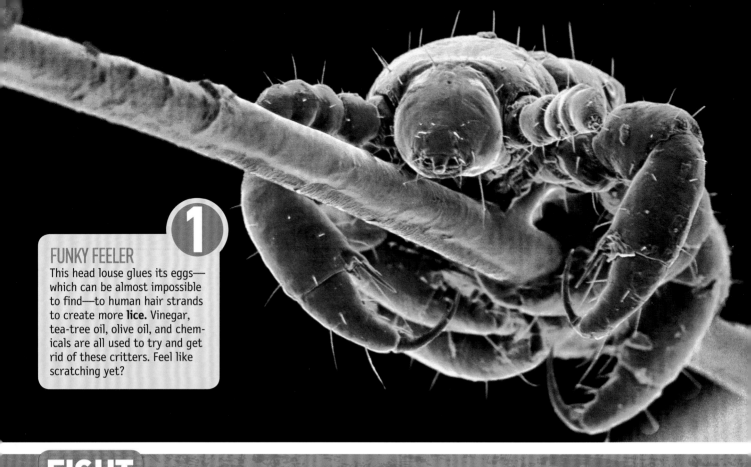

FUNKY FEELER

1

This head louse glues its eggs—which can be almost impossible to find—to human hair strands to create more **lice.** Vinegar, tea-tree oil, olive oil, and chemicals are all used to try and get rid of these critters. Feel like scratching yet?

EIGHT

CREEPIEST MICROSCOPIC CRITTERS

THEY'RE NOT AS BIG AS THEY LOOK! THESE PHOTOS, TAKEN USING A FOCUSED BEAM OF ELECTRONS, BRING OUT SOME OF THE DETAILS IN THE AIR YOU BREATHE AND THE CRITTERS THAT CAN MAKE YOUR BODY THEIR HOMES.

PRETTY POLLEN

2

With spiky spheres and dotted orbs, these **pollen grains,** with colors added to highlight their differences, look like treats in an exotic candy dish. Some are too small to be seen with the naked eye, but the largest pollen grains can be about as thick as a dollar bill.

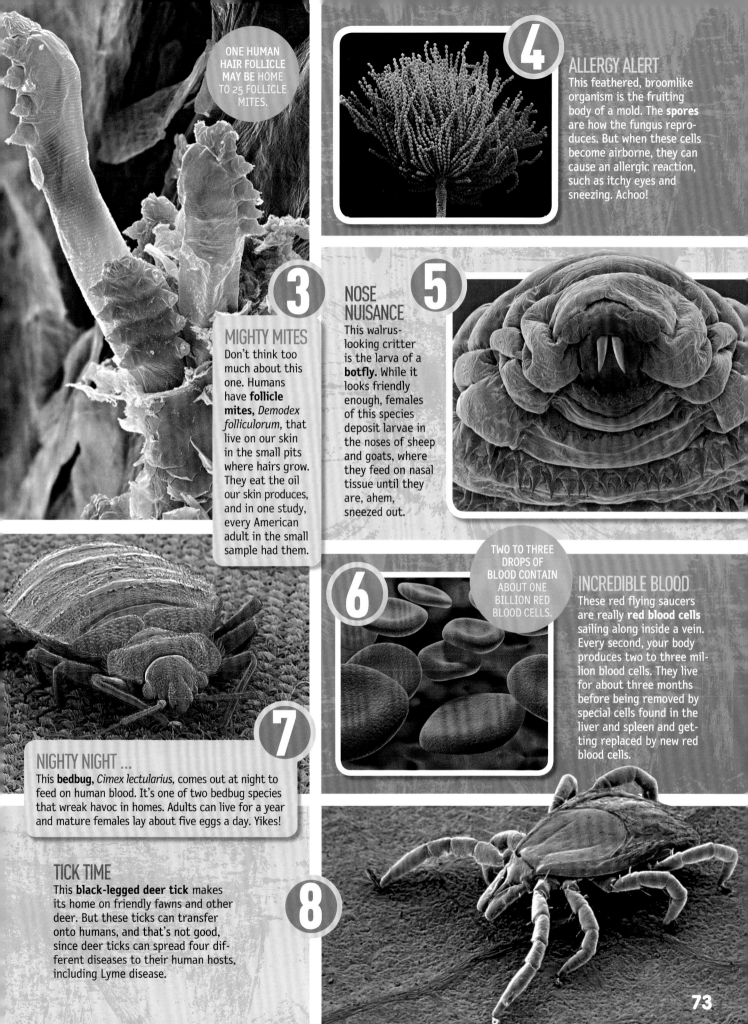

ONE HUMAN HAIR FOLLICLE MAY BE HOME TO 25 FOLLICLE MITES.

4 ALLERGY ALERT

This feathered, broomlike organism is the fruiting body of a mold. The **spores** are how the fungus reproduces. But when these cells become airborne, they can cause an allergic reaction, such as itchy eyes and sneezing. Achoo!

3 MIGHTY MITES

Don't think too much about this one. Humans have **follicle mites**, *Demodex folliculorum*, that live on our skin in the small pits where hairs grow. They eat the oil our skin produces, and in one study, every American adult in the small sample had them.

5 NOSE NUISANCE

This walrus-looking critter is the larva of a **botfly.** While it looks friendly enough, females of this species deposit larvae in the noses of sheep and goats, where they feed on nasal tissue until they are, ahem, sneezed out.

TWO TO THREE DROPS OF BLOOD CONTAIN ABOUT ONE BILLION RED BLOOD CELLS.

INCREDIBLE BLOOD

These red flying saucers are really **red blood cells** sailing along inside a vein. Every second, your body produces two to three million blood cells. They live for about three months before being removed by special cells found in the liver and spleen and getting replaced by new red blood cells.

6

7 NIGHTY NIGHT ...

This **bedbug,** *Cimex lectularius*, comes out at night to feed on human blood. It's one of two bedbug species that wreak havoc in homes. Adults can live for a year and mature females lay about five eggs a day. Yikes!

TICK TIME

This **black-legged deer tick** makes its home on friendly fawns and other deer. But these ticks can transfer onto humans, and that's not good, since deer ticks can spread four different diseases to their human hosts, including Lyme disease.

8

Eye-Opening
ANCIENT MYSTERIES

THESE MYSTERIES FROM HISTORY ARE COLD CASES WAITING TO BE SOLVED.

COLOSSAL HEADS ①

The Olmec people of Mesoamerica vanished around 300 B.C., and no one knows why. They left something huge behind, though: more than a dozen of these **carved stone heads,** which are as tall as 11 feet (3.4 m) and weigh 20 tons (18 t) each. Experts believe the heads are portraits of Olmec rulers.

MYSTERY LANGUAGE

The ancient people of Easter Island once possessed written language in the form of hieroglyphic scripts called **Rongorongo.** The script hasn't been deciphered, in part because when Europeans colonized the island, they destroyed most examples of it.

2

MYSTERIOUS MANUSCRIPT

The **Voynich Manuscript** has puzzled researchers ever since it came to the public's attention in 1912, when book dealer Wilfrid M. Voynich bought it in Italy. The handwritten pages, which date back to the 1400s, contain botanical drawings, although no one has been able to identify what the plants are. And no one has been able to decode the language the book is written in.

3

THE GREAT SPHINX MAY HAVE ONCE BEEN COVERED IN COLORFUL PAINT.

4

LOST CITY

Excavations in Turkey in the late 19th century revealed that the **city of Troy,** once thought to be an imaginary city from Homer's ancient poem *The Iliad,* actually existed. Archaeologists are searching for clues about the kingdom and whether it was conquered during the Trojan War, as the 3,000-year-old legend says.

5

UNCREDITED MONUMENT

For being such a massive monument, no one knows for sure who made the **Great Sphinx of Giza.** Some believe it was Khafre, who ruled ancient Egypt 4,600 years ago; others believe it was Khafre's father, who oversaw the building of the Great Pyramid of Giza.

MYTHICAL LAND

More than 2,000 years ago, the Greek philosopher Plato wrote about **Atlantis,** a legendary island in the Atlantic Ocean filled with gold, silver, and exotic animals. The story says that Atlantis eventually sank into the sea after being destroyed by fires and earthquakes—the gods punishing its inhabitants.

6

8

CIRCLE OF STONES

Scientists have been examining **Stonehenge,** a 5,000-year-old monument in southern England, for centuries. Folklore says Merlin, the wizard, created it by moving the giant stones from Ireland. Theories today say it might have been a holy site or celestial observatory.

7

A COLONY VANISHED

More than 100 colonists who settled on **Roanoke Island,** North Carolina, U.S.A., in 1587 disappeared without a trace three years later. The only clues left behind were the words "Croatoan" carved into a gatepost of their fort and "Cro" scratched into a tree. No one knows for sure where they vanished to.

TURN THE PAGE TO SEE HOW A DIFFERENT "HENGE" STACKS UP.

CURIOUS CARHENGE

THIS SCULPTURE PUTS A NEW SPIN ON AN ANCIENT WONDER.

EIGHT FAB REPLICAS OF FAMOUS PLACES

① Mount Rushmore in China
A smaller version of the soaring South Dakota, U.S.A., presidential mountainside monument was sculpted in Chongqing, China.

② Taj Mahal in Bangladesh
A full-scale copy of the famous mausoleum and World Heritage site was built here for residents who can't undertake the expensive trip to see the original in India.

③ The Edible White House
Yum! In 2012, White House pastry chef Bill Yosses made a 300-pound (136-kg) White House gingerbread replica with more than 175 pounds (79 kg) of gingerbread and 50 pounds (23 kg) of chocolate.

④ Eiffel Tower in Texas
In Paris, Texas, U.S.A., a 65-foot (20-m) Eiffel Tower replica is topped with a cowboy hat.

We don't know much about the people who built Stonehenge, but there's no mystery behind who built Carhenge—or how he managed to do it. Artist Jim Reinders finished the remarkable replica in 1987, but the idea for it came five years earlier, when he and his family decided to build a memorial in honor of Reinders's father.

Reinders had studied Stonehenge when he was living in England and thought cars would make good stand-ins for those giant stones on Wiltshire, England's Salisbury Plain. So he got to work planning and figured out how to bring a little piece of prehistoric England to some property in Alliance, Nebraska, U.S.A.

It took 39 vintage cars, pickup trucks, and even an ambulance to replicate Stonehenge, creating a circle measuring 96 feet (29 m) in diameter. Some of the vehicles were placed in deep pits and others were welded together. To make them uniform, they were all painted with gray spray paint. It may not be the tourist destination that Stonehenge is, but Carhenge does draw thousands of visitors every year. It's free and open every day.

OTHER ARTISTS HAVE DONATED THEIR CAR CREATIONS TO REINDERS, AND THOSE SCULPTURES ARE NOW ON DISPLAY ON THE SAME PIECE OF FARMLAND, AT THE NEARBY CAR ART RESERVE.

Thousands of people flock to Stonehenge annually during summer solstice to see the sunrise. Summer solstice is the day that Earth's axis is most aligned with the sun, which provides the most daylight of the year. Traditionally, people have gathered and faced the northeasterly direction to watch the sun rise above Stonehenge's Heel Stone. In August 2017, something extra special happened at Carhenge: The monument was in the path of a total solar eclipse, and a celebration was thrown there in its honor. Instead of facing northeast, eclipse watchers donned special glasses and gazed at the moon passing between the sun and Earth.

Lego London At an amusement park in England, you can visit a miniature version of the streets of London—all built with Lego pieces!

⑤

Louvre Pyramid in China A replica of Paris, France's famous Louvre Pyramid greets visitors at a subway entrance in China.

⑥

Parthenon in Tennessee A Parthenon replica in Nashville, Tennessee, U.S.A., is the same size as the original in Greece.

⑦

Leaning Tower of Illinois A half-scale replica of Italy's Leaning Tower of Pisa can be found in Niles, Illinois, U.S.A.

⑧

EIGHT UPLIFTING HOT AIR BALLOONS

LOOK: UP IN THE SKY! IT'S A BIRD! IT'S A ... CAKE?! IT'S A ... DARTH VADER?! THESE HOT AIR BALLOONS FLOAT TO ALL NEW LEVELS OF EXTREME.

1 · A LOT OF HOT AIR

The **Flying Scotsman** is just that—a 156-foot (47.5-m)-tall bagpiper that flies through the skies. Dressed in traditional Scottish clothes, and captained by an actual Scotsman, the balloon is eye-catching but not aerodynamic or designed for long distances.

2 · WHERE ARE THE PIGS?

No slingshot needed: This **Angry Bird** floats through the Albuquerque International Balloon Fiesta without any green pigs in its way. At 80 feet (24 m), it was one of hundreds of balloons that took to the skies in 2014 at the annual event in New Mexico, U.S.A.

3 · FISH OUT OF WATER

This **fish** appears to be swimming through the blue—but that isn't water! It's blue skies. Amazingly, the first passengers to go up in a hot air balloon were animals. In 1783, a sheep, duck, and a rooster were the passengers aboard the first flight.

THE FIRST HUMAN IN A HOT AIR BALLOON TOOK FLIGHT TWO MONTHS AFTER THE ANIMALS DID—AND FLOATED ABOUT 5.5 MILES (9 KM).

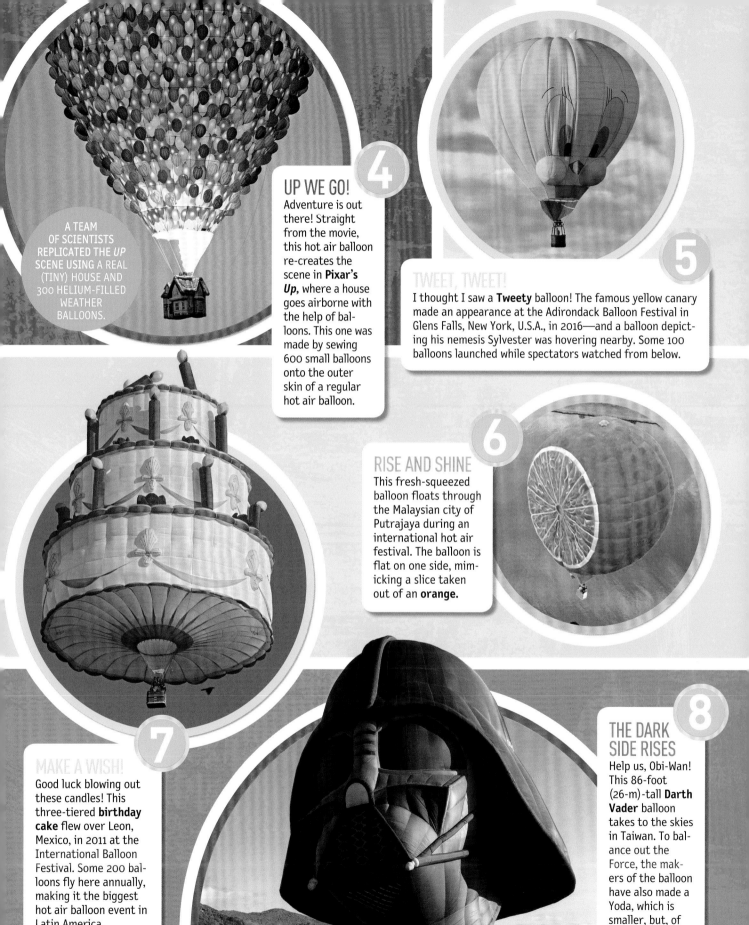

A TEAM OF SCIENTISTS REPLICATED THE *UP* SCENE USING A REAL (TINY) HOUSE AND 300 HELIUM-FILLED WEATHER BALLOONS.

4 UP WE GO!
Adventure is out there! Straight from the movie, this hot air balloon re-creates the scene in **Pixar's Up,** where a house goes airborne with the help of balloons. This one was made by sewing 600 small balloons onto the outer skin of a regular hot air balloon.

5 TWEET, TWEET!
I thought I saw a **Tweety** balloon! The famous yellow canary made an appearance at the Adirondack Balloon Festival in Glens Falls, New York, U.S.A., in 2016—and a balloon depicting his nemesis Sylvester was hovering nearby. Some 100 balloons launched while spectators watched from below.

6 RISE AND SHINE
This fresh-squeezed balloon floats through the Malaysian city of Putrajaya during an international hot air festival. The balloon is flat on one side, mimicking a slice taken out of an **orange.**

7 MAKE A WISH!
Good luck blowing out these candles! This three-tiered **birthday cake** flew over Leon, Mexico, in 2011 at the International Balloon Festival. Some 200 balloons fly here annually, making it the biggest hot air balloon event in Latin America.

8 THE DARK SIDE RISES
Help us, Obi-Wan! This 86-foot (26-m)-tall **Darth Vader** balloon takes to the skies in Taiwan. To balance out the Force, the makers of the balloon have also made a Yoda, which is smaller, but, of course, just as mighty.

1

ROBIN HOOD'S HANGOUT
According to folklore, this 1,000-year-old oak tree in England's Sherwood Forest is the legendary hideaway for Robin Hood and his Merry Men. Known as **Major Oak**, it is the biggest oak tree in Britain. In a good year, the tree produces around 150,000 acorns.

EIGHT
WEIRD AND WONDERFUL
TREES
OLD, TALL, GNARLY, AND SURREAL—THESE ARE NOT YOUR EVERYDAY TREES.

2

SUPER SOLAR
These "trees" are the ultimate multitaskers. Standing up to 164 feet (50 m) tall, the trees in Singapore's **Supertree Grove** are sculptures covered in living plants, making them look like real trees. Their massive canopies provide shade for pedestrians during the day, and in the evening they glow with a solar-powered light display.

THE TREES' RED RESIN HAS BEEN USED IN DYES AND MEDICINE FOR THOUSANDS OF YEARS.

3 A TREE THAT BLEEDS

It looks like an umbrella, it acts like an umbrella, but it's actually a **dragon's blood tree.** Native to the islands off the Horn of Africa, this slow-growing tree gets its name from the red resin that drips from the bark if it is cut.

4 ICE AGE TREE

This may very well be the oldest living tree on Earth. Discovered in Sweden, the **spruce's** root system has been growing since the end of the last ice age—9,550 years ago. How? After its trunk dies, a new one grows from the same root stock, allowing it to stand the test of time.

5 NATURE VS. ARCHITECTURE

Don't underestimate the power of a tree. This **untamed tree** is taking over a corner of the famous Angkor Wat temple complex in Cambodia! Found in Asia and parts of Australia, *Tetrameles nudiflora* can grow to 150 feet (46 m) tall, regardless of what's in its path.

6 WORLD'S TALLEST TREE

You'd think you could find the world's tallest tree, named **Hyperion,** pretty easily. But its location—somewhere in Humboldt Redwoods State Park in California, U.S.A.—is kept quiet to make sure it isn't damaged. (Scientists have climbed it and measured it.) The coast redwood stands at an incredible 369 feet (112.5 m)—taller than the Statue of Liberty.

7 THE UPSIDE-DOWN TREE

They might look straight out of a Dr. Seuss book, but these **baobab trees** that line a dirt road in the island nation of Madagascar are the real deal. With their wide smooth trunks and limbs that resemble roots popping up at the top, at first glance you might think they were growing upside down!

FRUIT FROM BAOBAB TREES IS USED TO MAKE A SWEET-AND-SOUR-TASTING JUICE.

8 OPEN-AIR MUSEUM

Art meets nature in the **Oma Forest,** located in Spain's Basque Country. Painter and sculptor Agustin Ibarrola painted colorful patterns, shapes, and figures on pine trees, combining techniques from the Paleolithic period as well as the modern era.

EIGHT
MEGA-EXTREME SPORTS THAT CATCH AIR

YOU'D BETTER LIKE HEIGHTS IF YOU PLAY ANY OF THESE SPORTS ... BECAUSE THE SKY REALLY IS THE LIMIT!

AT 4'9", SIMONE BILES WAS THE SHORTEST OF ALL THE ATHLETES AT THE 2016 OLYMPIC GAMES.

DEFYING GRAVITY

Considered the world's best gymnast, American Simone Biles can leap, twist, and flip like no other. At the 2016 Olympics, she won four gold medals and a bronze, and she even has her own move: **the Biles.** It's a double flip with a half-twist and ends in a blind landing.

2

ALLEY-OOP!

Now here's a way to guarantee a dunk—**trampoline basketball,** or basketball with some assists by trampolines. Sometimes going by the name SlamBall, the game has been picking up speed with the popularity of indoor trampoline parks.

1

DIVE IN!

Look out below! This **cliff diver** takes a big leap in Mazatlán, Mexico. People have been cliff diving for centuries. It is said that Hawaiian warriors jumped from a cliff on the island of Lanai to prove their loyalty and bravery.

3

GO FLY A KITE

4

Now here's how to catch some air! A kiteboarder uses the wind to his advantage on the waters off the island-nation of Mauritius, in the Indian Ocean. **Kiteboarders** are able to move along the water and make jumps up to 50 feet (15 m) by using strength and coordination to control the kite that they're attached to.

FLIGHT OF THE FUTURE

5

Hoverboards may seem old school once jetpacks or flyboards (like the one shown here) hit the mainstream. Still in development, **Flyboard Air** has four engines, operates by a handheld remote, and is fueled by kerosene. It will be able to cover more than 7,000 feet (2,134 m) without stopping. Up, up, and away!

SPRINGS FOR FEET

6

This super bouncer from California, U.S.A., can jump more than six feet (1.8 m) in the air on his **pogo stick.** Traditionally, pogo sticks get their bounce from springs, but this one works with compressed air, which increases height.

A MAN HOPPING ON A POGO STICK COMPLETED A MARATHON IN 16 HOURS AND 24 MINUTES.

OFF THE WALL

7

You literally bounce off the walls when doing this extreme sport! Part gymnastics, park parkour, **wall trampoline** jumpers improvise in mid-flight. Cirque du Soleil acrobats have been doing a version of wall trampoline for years during their performances, and it has since gone mainstream.

FLIPPING OUT

8

American Cameron Zink does the biggest step-down backflip in history, shown in these images spliced together, at a 2013 freeride mountain bike competition in Utah, U.S.A. **Freeride mountain biking** sends riders down routes that look impossible to most people. Besides trails, they ride on wood planks, platforms—even off cliffs!

MOST OFFBEAT CHAIRS

GET READY TO KICK BACK AND RELAX IN SOME OF THE MOST FANTASTICAL CHAIRS IN THE WORLD.

IF AN OCTOPUS LOSES AN ARM, IT CAN REGROW ANOTHER.

2 CEPHALOPOD SEATER

This mollusk masterpiece brings the sea to your seat. Spanish artist Máximo Riera created this artistic **octopus chair** as part of his animal chair collection, which also includes a beetle chair and a toad chair, as well as mammals from whales to hippos.

1 MUSICAL CHAIRS

This outdoor art exhibit presents **trees as an orchestra** ready to "play" Vivaldi's musical piece, *The Four Seasons*, in the middle of a Belgian forest. The trees change over the four seasons. Twenty-five chairs host trees, and one is left open for a human visitor.

5 CHA-CHING

Ever wonder the best way to handle loose change? You could put it in a bank, in a parking meter, or ... in a chair! A slew of coins welded together make for one sensational **silver seat.**

4 MAMMOTH ROCKER

It would take a pretty big giant to rock in this 56-foot (17-m)-tall behemoth, the world's largest **rocking chair.** It took 10 regular-size people to move the 46,200-pound (20,955-kg) wood-and-steel rocker into its place in Casey, Illinois, U.S.A. The enormous project took two years to complete.

CASEY ALSO SHOWCASES A GIANT MAILBOX, OVERSIZE WOODEN SHOES, A HUGE PITCHFORK, AND OTHER OVERLY LARGE OBJECTS.

8 CRAZY CLASSROOM

A field in Hampstead Heath in London, England, transformed into a giant classroom when this 30-foot (9-m)-tall artwork, titled **"The Writer,"** arrived. The Italian artist, a former soccer player, suggested that viewers use the table legs as goalposts. Score!

THE SCULPTURE USED 1,000 POUNDS (454 KG) OF WOOD AND SIX TONS (5.4 T) OF STEEL.

7 FOREST THRONE

St. Patrick's Chair in the People's Millennium Forest in Northern Ireland is taller than most people—6.5 feet (2 m). Legend has it that Druids—ancient Celtic priests and leaders—met around this natural stone throne until St. Patrick drove them out in the fifth century A.D.

3 MOTO-LOUNGER

This **motorized lounger** puts a whole new spin on being an armchair traveler! Since 2005, Armchair Cruisers has been modifying chairs into freewheeling machines able to reach speeds of 50 miles an hour (80 km/h). But you might want to start saving any coins that fall under the cushion—these chairs can cost as much as $10,000.

6 BEACH SEAT

It would be impossible to miss this dynamic **deck chair** hanging out on a sandy beach! But you might have to pack a ladder along with your sunblock.

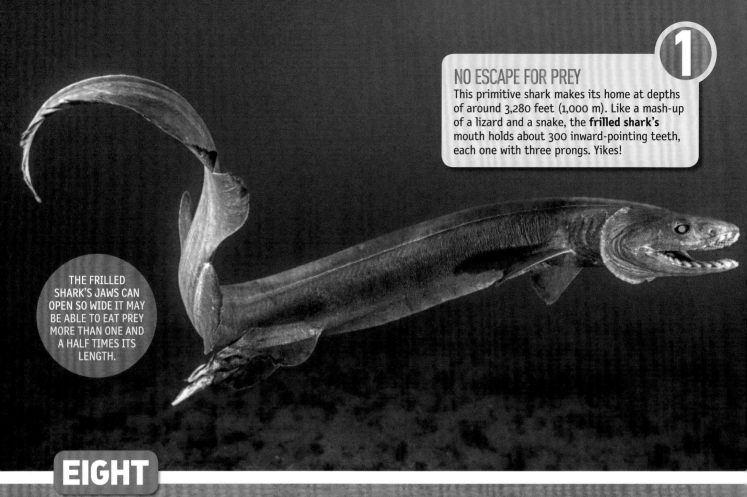

1

NO ESCAPE FOR PREY

This primitive shark makes its home at depths of around 3,280 feet (1,000 m). Like a mash-up of a lizard and a snake, the **frilled shark's** mouth holds about 300 inward-pointing teeth, each one with three prongs. Yikes!

THE FRILLED SHARK'S JAWS CAN OPEN SO WIDE IT MAY BE ABLE TO EAT PREY MORE THAN ONE AND A HALF TIMES ITS LENGTH.

EIGHT
ODDEST DEEP-SEA CREATURES

FOR THESE UNDER-THE-RADAR ANIMALS, PECULIAR ADAPTATIONS ARE ROUTINE.

2

COLOSSAL CRUSTACEAN

The **giant isopod** could star in a sci-fi movie! The crustacean, which can be more than one foot (0.3 m) long, lives at depths of more than 2,000 feet (610 m). To protect its soft belly, it will roll itself into a ball.

GIANT ISOPODS CAN SURVIVE FOR YEARS WITHOUT EATING.

TOTALLY TUBULAR (4)

These giant **tube worms** like it hot! They thrive near hydrothermal vents on the Pacific Ocean floor. The vents release toxic superheated chemicals where the seafloor is spreading apart. But the worms don't mind—that is, unless an undersea eruption wipes out the whole colony.

BRIGHT LIGHTS (5)

The **vampire squid** may be small, only about six inches (15 cm) in length, but it has one supersize talent. Special organs called photophores give this squid the ability to light up. It can even change its patterns to attract prey or confuse predators.

EAR FLAPS (3)

The **Dumbo octopus** looks like an underwater version of the famous flying elephant with superlarge ears. Its "ears" are actually fins that the creature flaps to help it swim at depths of at least 13,100 feet (4,000 m).

THERE ARE AROUND 200 SPECIES OF LANTERN-FISH, MAKING THEM ONE OF THE MOST COMMON FISH IN THE DEEP SEA.

GLOW FISH (7)

It's easy to see how this big-eyed critter got its name. This **Chaves' lanternfish** also uses photophores to produce light, seen here as glowing stripes near its tail and as white dots on its belly.

CRAZY CRAWLER (6)

Diver Eugenie Clark examines a giant **Japanese spider crab** off Japan's Izu Peninsula. The largest known living crab, its outstretched legs can span 13 feet (4 m). The crab isn't a fearsome hunter, though: It snacks on dead animal matter.

FABULOUS FANGS (8)

The **Pacific viperfish** has chompers so long they don't even fit into its mouth! Scientists think the petite predator rushes at its victims and impales them on its teeth. Its fearsome look makes up for its smallish size; it's only about a foot (30 cm) long.

EIGHT
Out-of-This-World
IMAGES

THESE COSMICALLY COOL PICTURES UNCOVER THE WONDER OF THE UNIVERSE.

① SUPERNOVA REMNANTS

This mosaic of six images from NASA's Hubble Space Telescope shows an area of the **Veil Nebula** about two light-years across. (The whole nebula is 110 light-years across.) The wispy gas trails are all that's left of an ancient star that was once 20 times more massive than our sun.

A MOUNTAIN RANGE ON PLUTO RISES AS HIGH AS 11,000 FEET (3,500 M).

DWARF PLANET

NASA's New Horizons spacecraft captured this image of **Pluto** (in the foreground) and its moon Charon. The colors here are made by combining three different images, and while the relative sizes are close to accurate, the relative distance apart is not to scale.

TELESCOPE POWER

Two small dwarf galaxies known as the Magellanic Clouds can be seen above one of the telescopes at the **Paranal Observatory** in the Atacama Desert in northern Chile. The observatory is home to the Very Large Telescope.

THE FIRST IMAGE OF AN EXOPLANET WAS CAPTURED BY THE VERY LARGE TELESCOPE.

RING WORLD

A close-up of Saturn's **expansive ring system**, highlighted with different colors, shows its elaborate structures. Rings are made up of millions of fragments of ice and rock, and have gaps inside containing ringlets. Other rings have moons embedded within them. The Voyager 2 spacecraft took this image in 1981.

MEGASIZE EARTH

This "super Earth" (seen here in an artist's rendering) is more than five times as massive as our home planet and orbits a red dwarf star about 33 light-years away. Supersize aliens aren't hanging out here, though, as scientists think exoplanet **GJ 536b** is too close to its star to be habitable.

BLAZING WORLD

An artist's rendition of **Kepler 20e** shows the rocky exoplanet with active volcanoes. The exoplanet is much too hot to support life as we know it, with surface temperatures thought to be 1400°F (760°C), or about four times hotter than an oven baking a cake. Burn!

BLACK AND WHITE

Iapetus, Saturn's third largest moon, appears as a pockmarked gumball. This image is highlighted to make the colors more pronounced, but the moon really is two-toned. Small dust particles from another of Saturn's moons, Phoebe, accumulate on the dark side but not on the icy white side.

EXTREME EXOPLANET

This NASA illustration shows the exoplanet **HD 189733 b,** located some 63 light-years away from Earth in the constellation Vulpecula. This planet may look friendly, but don't be fooled: Winds howl here at 5,400 miles an hour (8,700 km/h)—seven times the speed of sound!—and it likely rains molten glass.

TURN THE PAGE FOR MORE ON SPACE!

AN ARTIST'S RENDERING OF THE SPUTNIK 1 SPACE-CRAFT IN ORBIT AROUND EARTH.

EIGHT STUNNING SPACE MISSIONS

① Apollo 13
Although this mission was intended to be the third to reach the moon, a malfunction prevented the crew from reaching the lunar surface. Their safe return to Earth against all odds, however, made them heroes the world over.

② Mariner 4
In July 1965, the space probe Mariner 4 took 21 black-and-white pictures as it passed by the red planet—our first pictures of Mars.

③ Voyager 2 A gold-plated record containing different sounds from around the world was carried on both the Voyager 1 and Voyager 2 space probes, both launched in 1977. The record was a way to introduce our world to any extraterrestrial that might be listening!

④ Spirit Rover
Launched in June 2003, this overachieving rover explored Martian geography for evidence of water. Spirit's original mission, planned for just 90 days, lasted until May 2009 when the roaming rover got stuck in soft soil.

CHARTING THE FINAL FRONTIER

HOW HUMANS HAVE EXPLORED THE UNIVERSE ... AND WHAT'S NEXT ON THE HORIZON

The same impulse that drove our ancestors to gaze into the night sky lives on today. But while the ancients could only daydream about space travel, humans have been actively developing the technology to help get us up there for the past six decades.

The space age began in 1957 when the Soviet Union launched Sputnik 1, the world's first artificial satellite, into orbit. Only a few years later, in 1961, Soviet cosmonaut Yuri Gagarin became the first human in space. And less than a decade later, on July 20, 1969, Apollo 11 astronauts Neil Armstrong and Edwin "Buzz" Aldrin took their first steps on the moon.

Early efforts such as Skylab in the 1970s and the Russian Mir orbiting space station in the 1980s and 1990s gave researchers the chance to study not only what happens to the human body in space but also how to live in space. And 20 years to the day after Gagarin was launched into orbit, the space shuttle *Columbia* took off from NASA's Kennedy Space Center. Shuttles would fly for 30 years on 135 missions. These missions and today's astronauts on the International Space Station continue to run experiments to learn more about living in space. Besides sending humans to space, we have gathered information using space probes, orbiters, and landers that fly past or orbit planets, asteroids, and even our sun.

So, what's next? Today, scientists, CEOs, and wannabe space explorers have their sights set on our nearest planetary neighbor: Mars. Walking on the moon is an amazing accomplishment, but living on Mars—about 36 million miles (58 million km) away at its closest—would be quite another. How would explorers survive in the harsh conditions? What would they eat? Robotic rovers have already landed on Mars, tooling around to explore the landscape.

NASA and private space companies are working to send humans to the red planet by the 2030s. Some first steps include a yearlong mission into deep space, and capturing an asteroid that will then be put into orbit around our moon so that astronauts can be sent to explore it. One thing is for sure: The sky is definitely no longer the limit.

Cassini-Huygens 5
The Huygens probe landed on Saturn's largest moon, Titan, in January 2005 to record the first-ever images of the moon's surface—where temperatures are hundreds of degrees below freezing. *Brrr.*

OSIRIS-REx 6
Launched in 2016, NASA's OSIRIS-REx mission is traveling to the asteroid Bennu to collect samples and return the "aster-rocks" back to Earth in 2023.

Ulysses 7 This far-out mission was launched from the *Discovery* space shuttle in October 1990. Ten instruments on board the Ulysses space probe measured the effects the sun and solar wind has on our solar system. The mission lasted more than 18 years and included nearly three complete orbits around the sun.

New Horizons 8 New Horizons became the first mission to fly by Pluto in July 2015. Now, it's on its way to an object even farther away, 2014 MU69, in the region known as the Kuiper belt.

EIGHT

BOLD AND BRIGHT BIRDS

IN A COMPETITION OF THE MOST BRILLIANT FEATHERS, THESE BIRDS WOULD WIN WITH FLYING COLORS!

ROYAL HUNTER

There's nothing common about the **common kingfisher.** This species stands apart with its iridescent blue feathers. Kingfishers are often found near water, where they hunt for and eat more than half their body weight every day, mostly in the form of small fish.

2

QUETZAL FEATHERS WERE A SYMBOL OF WEALTH IN ANCIENT MAYA AND AZTEC SOCIETIES.

RAINBOW BRIGHT

Widespread throughout Australia, **rainbow lorikeets** tend to gather in a loud, communal roost at dusk and eat flowers, fruits, and seeds during the day. The tip of their tongue has fine hairs to collect nectar.

1

BIRDS OF A FEATHER

This inhabitant of the mountains of Central America has long been prized for its feathers. It takes three years for a male **resplendent quetzal** to grow its tail feathers, which can flow as long as three feet (1 m).

3

SHOW-OFF

There are dozens of species of **birds of paradise,** but what they all have in common is their brilliant colors and exceptional tail feathers. To attract females, male birds of paradise perform elaborate dances, hopping back and forth and bobbing their heads.

5

4

SEEING RED

If the **northern cardinal** looks familiar, it may be because it's the official bird of seven U.S. states and the mascot of a major league baseball team. Only the eye-catching males are red; females are tan and gray.

RAINBOW OF COLOR

7

This **fiery-throated hummingbird** can check off just about every color of the rainbow. Found in the cloud forests of Costa Rica, it's iridescent feathers make its throat glimmer in the sunlight. Like all hummingbirds, its rapid wingbeats—up to 100 per second—make a humming sound.

6

PARADISE ON EARTH

As colorful as a painter's palette, the **paradise tanager** lives in the Amazon basin, streaking through the canopy with its apple-green and blue markings. It usually hangs out in groups of 5 to 10 and eats mostly fruits and some insects and spiders.

BABY PEAFOWL ARE CALLED PEACHICKS.

8

LOOK AT ME!

It's hard not to notice a **peacock** when it puts its feathers on full display. Its train of feathers makes up 60 percent of its total body length! Only males are called peacocks; females are called peahens, and together they are peafowl. Peafowl have been kept as pets for centuries.

1

FLYING HIGH

On May 21, 1932, **Amelia Earhart** became the first woman to fly solo across the Atlantic Ocean when she landed her Lockheed Vega plane in Northern Ireland. During her 15-hour flight, Earhart drank tomato juice and ate chocolate to keep herself fueled.

> AS A CHILD, AMELIA HAD A LARGE BLACK DOG NAMED JAMES FEROCIOUS.

EIGHT
EXTRAORDINARY JOURNEYS

THESE BRAVE AND GRITTY EXPLORERS BATTLED HIGH SEAS, UNFORGIVING ICE, AND MILES OF FOREIGN TERRAIN ON THEIR EPIC ADVENTURES.

2

MOON SHOT

Neil Armstrong took this picture of **Edwin "Buzz" Aldrin** during the 1969 Apollo 11 mission to the moon. The NASA astronauts were the first of only 12 men ever to walk on the moon. The lunar lander, the *Eagle*, can be seen at left.

FANTASTIC VOYAGES

4

To extend naval power, Chinese Admiral **Zheng He** (ca 1371–1433) sailed the Indian Ocean during seven far-reaching expeditions. And his journeys were massive! On his first journey, in 1405, he took 62 ships and 27,800 men to India and Sri Lanka.

HEADING WEST

3

Sacagawea shows **Meriwether Lewis and William Clark** the way during their epic journey across thousands of miles of the American West. In November 1804, Sacagawea, a Shoshone Indian, and her French-Canadian husband joined up to translate for the group as they encountered American Indians.

EXTREME ENDURANCE

5

Polar explorer **Ernest Shackleton's** ice-encrusted boat, *Endurance*, became stuck in January 1915 during his attempt to lead the first team to cross Antarctica. The ship sank, but the entire crew was saved after a year and a half, thanks to Shackleton's heroic efforts.

PHOTOGRAPHER FRANK HURLEY DOCUMENTED THE FRIGID ADVENTURE USING BOTH A FILM AND A MOVIE CAMERA.

SCOTT'S TEAM ARRIVED JUST ONE MONTH AFTER AMUNDSEN'S—AND PERISHED ON THEIR TREK BACK TO BASE CAMP.

7

DRESSED FOR ACTION

The race to reach the South Pole between Norwegian **Roald Amundsen** (pictured here) and British explorer Robert Falcon Scott was a tale for the ages. Amundsen and his team reached the South Pole first, on December 14, 1911.

ROAMING RAFT

6

In 1947, Norwegian explorer Thor Heyerdahl set out from Peru in a simple, balsa-wood raft to show how ancient peoples could have crossed the Pacific Ocean. The voyage ended after 101 days at sea when the raft, the *Kon-Tiki,* shipwrecked the crew on a Polynesian island. (They were rescued.)

WORLD TRAVELER

8

Even before airplanes, distance was no object for **Ibn Battuta**, a 14th-century Arab explorer. He traveled over some 75,000 miles (120,000 km) throughout the Middle East, along the African coast, and into India and China. His travel records help historians understand the Muslim world of his time.

ELABORATE EATERIES

FROM UNDERWATER BISTROS TO SENSORY SMORGASBORDS, THE FOOD AT THESE UNBELIEVABLE RESTAURANTS IS ALMOST SECOND TO THE EXPERIENCE OF DINING AT THEM.

2

AERIAL EATS

Afraid of heights? You might want to pull your chair up to a different table. Extreme thrills and fine dining meet at **Dinner in the Sky,** where plates are served on a platform 130 feet (40 m) in the air. This intense experience has been set up in more than 40 countries.

1

FAR OUT!

The **Alain Ducasse au Plaza Athénée** in Paris, France, is named after its famous chef. But eating in this glamorous setting isn't the only way to enjoy Alain Ducasse's creations. He also created tuna with lemon sauce and spiced chicken dishes for astronauts on the International Space Station.

ITHAA IS THE WORLD'S LARGEST AQUARIUM TUNNEL. THE RESTAURANT ARRIVED ON A BARGE AFTER 16 DAYS OF TRAVEL AT SEA.

3

SUBMERGED BISTRO

Over there we have ... a shark! At the **Ithaa restaurant** in the Maldives, that warning would come from an excited friend or waiter instead of a lifeguard. Located 10 feet (3 m) under the Indian Ocean, the restaurant's five-inch (125-mm)-thick acrylic keeps the sharks at arm's length.

4

FLOATING FEAST

At the **Sea Cloud** restaurant, guests dine on a five-course meal or a family BBQ while gazing out over the Indian Ocean. Located on the island nation of Mauritius, around 500 miles (800 km) off the coast of eastern Africa, this eatery is sea-sational.

5

DOWN-UNDER DELIGHT

Camping in the **Australian outback** might sound rustic, but at this five-star eco-camp, visitors nosh on pickled cabbage, free-range chicken, or honey sorbet as they look out over the heart of Australia.

6

ROOM WITH A VIEW(S)

The experience of eating a meal at **Sublimotion** on the island of Ibiza, Spain, never gets boring. The room turns into different scenes to complement the 20-course meal. Diners can eat in an orchard where every-thing is edible and then head off to the North Pole by dessert.

7

LIGHTS, CAMERA, FOOD

Eating at **Ultraviolet** in Shanghai, China, isn't simply a meal; it's a total sensory experience. Executive Chef Paul Pairet designed his restaurant—which consists of only a single table surrounded by video screen walls—to be a dining delight in which every course captures a different scene (and taste!) with music and video.

8

MUSICAL MEAL

For some theatergoers at the **Hungarian State Opera House** in Budapest, Hungary, the food takes center stage. Through a special arrangement with a local hotel, diners enjoy the theater all to themselves as they dine to classical music.

SUIT OF ARMOR

Don't mess with this distant relative of the armadillo. *Glyptotherium,* which lived four million to 10,000 years ago, had a serious shield against predators: Its hard shell was covered in spiked scales and was the size of a small car!

EIGHT INTRIGUING

THESE PREHISTORIC CREATURES SPORTED SOME CURIOUS CHARACTERISTICS.

ANCIENT ANIMALS

DEADLY BITE

Thylacoleo, the largest known carnivorous mammal in Australia, which went extinct about 45,000 years ago, had sharp teeth and a powerful bite. It was also a marsupial; newborns stayed in their mother's pouch. *Thylacoleo* ran on four legs but may have been able to stand on two.

MEGA ANTLERS

This giant deer, which lived as long as two million years ago, was the largest deer species to walk the Earth—its antlers spanned a whopping 12 feet (3.7 m)! *Megaloceros's* nickname, "Irish elk," comes from the many well preserved specimens found in lake beds and peat bogs on the Emerald Isle.

4

TINY PRIMATE

Weighing just one ounce (30 g), **Tinimomys** was tinier than the smallest primates living today. In fact, it was so small it could have sat on the end of your nose! *Tinimomys* lived about 56 million years ago at a time when mammals were still relatively compact.

3

5

WHAT BIG TEETH YOU HAVE

It certainly looks part rhinoceros and part saber-toothed cat, but *Uintatherium*, an herbivore, is not related to either. The hoofed animal, which lived 56 to 34 million years ago, had three pairs of horns and extra-large upper canine teeth. It stood about the same height as today's rhino.

CAN'T HOP TO IT

Sthenurus, a giant short-faced member of the kangaroo family, was three times as strong as a modern-day kangaroo. But that wasn't the biggest difference: This marsupial didn't hop. *Sthenurus*, which went extinct 30,000 years ago, walked on its hind feet.

7

STHENURUS MEANS "STRONG TAIL."

TALK TO THE HORN

6

Megacerops, a rhino-like grazer that roamed Earth 38 million years ago, was distinctive for its Y-shaped horn. Grazing on leaves and probably fruit, they were giants—standing more than eight feet (2.5 m) tall at the shoulder—but they had a very small brain.

ICE AGE RHINO

8

Coelodonta, also known as a "woolly rhino," looked like the rhinos that roam Africa today, but it was covered in fur. This was an adaptation to ice sweeping across Eurasia, where it lived as recently as 10,000 years ago.

EIGHT
MIGHTY MINIATURES

THESE ARTISTS MAKE A BIG SPLASH CREATING TINY THINGS.

CROME KNITS USING SURGICAL WIRE INSTEAD OF KNITTING NEEDLES.

2 TINY HAND WARMERS

These **hand-knitted gloves** may look pretty enough for a person, but they are better suited for a doll. Indiana, U.S.A.-based artist Althea Crome's creations are scaled to 1/12 of their normal size. She uses sewing thread, instead of yarn, and a lot of patience.

1 (TREE)HOUSE PLANT

You couldn't climb up to this tree house, but a house mouse certainly could! Los Angeles, California-based artist and propmaker Jedediah Corwyn Voltz incorporates his **mini-homes**—which he constructs from scraps of wood—into houseplants or bonsai trees.

3 SPOT OF TEA

This hand-thrown—or more like finger-thrown—tea kettle looks as detailed and perfect as its full-size counterpart, even though it's no bigger than playing dice. Washington State, U.S.A.-based sculptor Jon Almeda makes his **ceramics** on a motorized mini pottery wheel.

WIGAN USES HIS OWN PULSE AS A JACKHAMMER TO MOVE THE MATERIAL HE SCULPTS.

4 EYE OF THE BEHOLDER

This art demands a steady hand! These **itty-bitty sculptures** of the seasons are handmade by British artist Willard Wigan and then set into the eye of a needle. The sculptures are so tiny that they are best seen through a microscope!

5 DIFFERENT BALL OF WAX

This is one *golden* retriever! **Crayons** are typically used to make art—they aren't art all by themselves. But give artist Hoang Tran a crayon and a sculpting tool and he can turn that waxy stick into anything from dogs to *Star Wars* characters to superheroes.

6 MICRO EATS

This **teeny cake** looks good enough to eat! But alas, it's just made to look irresistible. Artist Stephanie Kilgast uses fine tools and a careful hand to craft her sculptures, which also include insects, sea creatures, and hybrid animals.

7 PURRFECT PETITE PORTRAIT

Steady there. Indiana, U.S.A.–based **watercolor artist** Brooke Rothshank cares about the little things. And with an ultrafine brush, she paints everything from animals, like this fingertip-size kitty, to everyday objects, which take her anywhere from 45 minutes to four hours to create.

8 A "PEEL"ING ART

Sweet ride! An artist who goes by the name Slinkachu customizes **miniature figurines** and then makes them appear bigger by positioning them next to full-size everyday objects. He places his scenes on the streets of London, England, for passersby to happen upon.

THE GOLDEN EAGLE THAT PERCHES ON AISHOLPAN'S ARM WEIGHS ABOUT THE SAME AS A JACK RUSSELL TERRIER.

1

EAGLE HUNTRESS

Aisholpan Nurgaiv, a teenage Kazakh girl living a nomadic life in Mongolia, is an **eagle hunter** (she trains her golden eagle to hunt), which is traditionally done by men. When she was 13 she won the prestigious eagle-hunters' competition held every year in the Mongolian town of Ölgiy.

EIGHT THINGS YOU MAY NOT KNOW ABOUT MONGOLIA

FROM FAMED FOSSILS TO FIERCE HUNTERS TO EXTREME OUTDOOR LIVING, MONGOLIA HONORS ITS HISTORY BY KEEPING THE PAST ALIVE.

2

DON'T DASH AWAY!

The **Dukha people**, who live in the forest of northern Mongolia, are nomadic reindeer herders, moving from pasture to pasture every 7 to 10 weeks. They even ride the reindeer like horses, with saddles! The reindeer are used for their milk.

FIERCE CONQUEROR

4

Mongolian warrior and ruler **Genghis Khan**, who lived in Mongolia 800 years ago, brought all of the nomadic tribes in northeast Asia under his rule and had an empire spanning Asia. His tactics for gaining territory were ruthless, but he also opened up contact between the East and West.

HARD TO SPOT

3

More **snow leopards** live in Mongolia than in any other country except China. Between 500 and 1,000 of the endangered large cats roam the mountains of Mongolia, but they are elusive, and researchers have a tough time tracking individuals. Snow leopards are also under threat from poaching and habitat loss.

NOT WHAT IT SEEMS

5

At 100 miles (161 km) long and up to 600 miles (966 km) wide, **the Gobi,** a desert in Mongolia and China, is the largest desert in Asia. But desert doesn't always mean hot: It can have subarctic winter temperatures.

GOBI MEANS "WATERLESS PLACE" IN MONGOLIAN.

POP-UP HOUSE

7

Imagine being able to assemble your house in less than an hour and then pack it up again and move on. This **yurt,** or *ger* in Mongolian, is a typical home for nomadic people. Its frame is made from lightweight wood and is covered in felt.

LAND OF THE HORSE

6

Mongolia remains a horse-based culture, and the nomadic people there continue to use them for travel, hunting, herding, and sport. **Horse racing** is a favorite sport among children, who learn to ride as jockeys as young as three years old.

FOREVER LOCKED IN BATTLE

8

The Gobi is rich with fossils, and one of the most famous found there is the **Fighting Dinosaurs**—a tussle between a *Velociraptor* and a *Protoceratops* frozen in time. Researchers believe they may have been buried by a landslide in the middle of their epic battle.

MOST ADORABLE ANIMAL
FAMILIES

WARNING: THE FURRY CUTIES ON THESE PAGES MAY CAUSE FITS OF JOY.

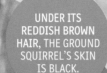

UNDER ITS REDDISH BROWN HAIR, THE GROUND SQUIRREL'S SKIN IS BLACK.

ANTARCTIC CUTIES

An adult **emperor penguin** hangs out with three cuddly chicks. When fully grown, these downy fluffballs can be 3.8 feet (1.2 m) tall. They'll have sleek feathers that keep them warm in frigid waters as they dive down as deep as 1,850 feet (564 m).

2

1

SAY CHEESE!

A group of South African **ground squirrels** appear to be posing for a family portrait. The species lives in burrows in the arid grasslands and savannas of southern Africa—even in the harsh Kalahari Desert.

ROLY-POLY

This **giant panda** mom and her cub have a grand time tumbling together. At birth, the cub was about the size of a stick of butter, but it will grow to be as large as 300 pounds (136 kg).

3

DOUBLE VISION

These **red-eyed tree frogs** live in Central America, where their striking colors may help protect them from predators. Female frogs lay their eggs on the underside of a leaf that hangs above a body of water, and when the tadpoles hatch they plop into the pond below.

4

FEMALE SEA OTTERS GIVE BIRTH IN THE WATER.

5

OTTER-LY CUTE

A newborn **sea otter** gets a ride—and a nuzzle—from its mom as it rides along on her belly in Prince William Sound in Alaska. The adorable aquatic mammals can be seen sleeping in large groups while floating on their backs.

6

MAMA BEAR

Polar bear cubs trail behind their mom in Wapusk National Park in Manitoba, Canada. While triplets are not as common as twins, all the cubs will stay with their mom for as long as three years while learning how to survive in their Arctic home.

NO ROADS (OR EVEN TRAILS!) LEAD INTO WAPUSK NATIONAL PARK.

7

FAMILY PORTRAIT

A young **quokka,** a type of small wallaby that only lives along a coastal stretch of Western Australia, sticks close to its mom. When fully grown, the furry mammal will be about the size of a house cat—and just as cute!

8

SIBLING JUMBLE

A **cheetah** mom watches over her eight-day-old cubs in Masai Mara National Reserve in Kenya. The dark "tear" marks beneath their eyes reflect the glare of the sun, which helps when the fastest land animal on Earth hunts during the day.

NEVER OPEN FOR BUSINESS

This 1,083-foot (330-m) pyramid-shaped hotel is the tallest structure in North Korea. Under construction since 1987, the **Ryugyong Hotel,** located in the capital city Pyongyang, has never officially opened.

ELEVATORS RUN UP THE CENTER OF THE BUILDING, CREATING A "DOUGHNUT" FLOOR PLAN.

2

BRIGHT LIGHTS

Barcelona, Spain's bullet-shaped **Torre Agbar** was designed to represent a water fountain that constantly changes its appearance. The 474-foot (144-m) tower's aluminum sheeting is made up of 40 different high-gloss colors, which change with the light. At night, more than 4,000 panels are illuminated, constantly rotating colors.

EIGHT

SERIOUSLY STEEP

THESE BUILDINGS ARE NOT ONLY SUPERTALL, THEY ARE ALSO ARCHITECTURAL WONDERS.

SKYSCRAPERS

106

3
A COCOON OF LEARNING

Tokyo, Japan's **Mode Gakuen Cocoon Tower** looks just like what its name implies: a cocoon. The 50-story educational facility was designed to symbolize a nurturing place for students before they head out into the world.

4
OLD MEETS NEW

Taipei 101, located in Taipei, Taiwan, stands 1,667 feet (508 m) tall, fusing modern, environmentally friendly engineering with Asian tradition. The building is shaped like a pagoda, and the eight sections of the building are intentional: Eight is a lucky number in Chinese culture.

TALLEST IN THE WEST

One World Trade Center, located in New York City, is the tallest building in the Western Hemisphere, measuring 1,776 feet (541 m)—a nod to the year of the signing of the U.S. Declaration of Independence. Its mirror-like window panels are like a kaleidoscope, changing throughout the day.

5

6
LOOKING SHARP

London's **The Shard**, also called the Shard of Glass because of its shape and sheen, is the tallest building in the U.K. Standing 1,004 feet (306 m), it is also considered a "vertical city," because it contains stores, offices, restaurants, and apartments.

TWISTY TOWER

The curved and spiraling design of the 2,073-foot (632-m) **Shanghai Tower**, located in Shanghai, China, symbolizes China emerging into the modern world. The design also helps offset high winds, which occur near the top of the building.

7
TWO HUNDRED WIND TURBINES AT THE TOP OF THE TOWER PRODUCE 10 PERCENT OF THE BUILDING'S ENERGY.

DOUBLE TALL

The 1,483-foot (452-m) **Petronas Towers** are twin skyscrapers located in Kuala Lumpur, Malaysia, that contain shopping centers, a museum, a symphony hall, a mosque, and a conference center. Each tower's floor plan forms an eight-pointed star, inspired by traditional Islamic patterns.

8

SPECTACULAR SNAPSHOTS OF **PARADISE**

TAKE A BREATHER, GRAB A SNACK, AND GET READY TO FEEL
THE WIND IN YOUR HAIR AND THE SAND BETWEEN YOUR TOES!

1 EDIBLE TREAT

What will you eat in paradise? These colorful sea creatures are actually a fruit called the **rambutan**! Commonly grown in Southeast Asia, the hairy rind, or outer skin, of this tropical snack encloses a soft, white fruit that tastes similar to a grape. The spikes are soft enough to bite into.

2 REMOTE WONDER

The palm trees, white sands, and crystal-clear waters of the **Aitutaki Lagoon** in the Cook Islands make it a postcardlike tropical getaway. The remote volcanic islands are located about halfway between Hawaii and New Zealand, in the South Pacific.

5 IN THE TREES

An aerial **tramway** in Costa Rica lets a biologist get up close to the forest canopy. Scientists think that around 60 to 90 percent of all rain forest life—like sloths, wild cats, monkeys, and frogs—can be found in the trees.

4 TURTLE TIME

Tropical seas offer endless opportunities to encounter sea life. A boy **snorkels** in the Red Sea off the coast of Egypt and happens upon a green turtle with a remora tagging along underneath. Remoras will catch a ride on turtles in part to eat their leftovers.

8 ALOHA AWESOMENESS

The rugged coastline of Hawaii's **Na Pali Coast** attracts adventurers who hanker for a remote escape. The 3,000-foot (910-m) cliffs create a natural fortress on the island of Kaua'i, but visitors can kayak, hike, helicopter, or raft into the paradise.

3 BLACK BEAUTY

The black sands of **Matavai Bay** beach in French Polynesia curve around the island paradise. When 18th-century explorer Captain James Cook first landed here, in 1769, he set up camp on the beach's east side, Point Venus.

AIRPLANE PILOTS FLYING OVER TROPICAL RAIN FORESTS HAVE SPOTTED BLUE MORPHOS FLYING ABOVE THE TREES.

7 BABY BLUE

The top of the wings of a **blue morpho** (*Morpho peleides*) butterfly shines an iridescent blue, while the undersides are drab brown. The blue adds a splash of color to the rain forest paradise, while the brown helps them blend in to keep hungry birds away.

6 WET WATERFALL

The milky spray of **La Mina Falls** in Puerto Rico can be reached by hiking a short 0.7-mile (1.1-km) rain forest trail. Located in the 29,000-acre (11,730-ha) El Yunque National Forest, the falls reward visitors with splashes in a crystal-clear pool and swims underneath the spray.

INDEX

PHOTO CREDITS

Cover: (chair), Jessica Bolin, Big Things Small Town; (Baobab trees), dennisvdw/iStock/Getty Images; (dolphin), Stephen Frink/The Image Bank/Getty Images; (purple amethyst), Enlightened Media/Alamy; (rainbow quartz), Tomatito/Shutterstock; (pink amethyst), Alexandr Parfenov/Alamy; (piglet), photomaster/Shutterstock; (ants), Rhonny Dayusasono/Caters News; **Back cover:** (mummified cat), The Natural History Museum/Alamy; (gecko), Kamonrat/Shutterstock; **Spine:** (piglet), photomaster/Shutterstock; 1 (CTR), Nazzu/Shutterstock; 2-3 (BACKGROUND), m-kojot/Getty Images; 4 (UP CTR), Kyle Huber; 4 (CTR LE), Tama-Chan, Simiiing Sushi Roll; 4 (CTR RT), Photo Insolite Realite/Science Photo Library/Getty Images; 4 (LO LE), Stuart G Porter/Shutterstock; 4 (LO RT), Marcos Delgado/Clasos.com/LatinContent/Getty Images; 6 (1), Rhonny Dayusasono/Caters News Agency; 6 (2), Bruno Nepomuceno/Caters News Agency; 6 (3), Ondrej Pakan/Caters News Agency; 7 (4), Darlyne A. Murawski/National Geographic Creative; 7 (5), Robin Moore/National Geographic Creative; 7 (6), Burak Senbak/Caters News Agency; 7 (7), Julian Ghahreman Rad/Caters News Agency; 7 (8), Mark Cowan/Caters News Agency; 8 (1), StockShot/Alamy; 8 (2), Oliver Furrer/Getty Images; 9 (3), Keith Ladzinski/National Geographic Creative; 9 (4), LucidSurf/Getty Images; 9 (5), Red Bull Content Pool/REX/Shutterstock; 9 (6), Christian Kober/Getty Images; 9 (7), COBi Digital; 9 (8), Oliver Furrer/agefotostock; 10 (1), Africa Studio/Shutterstock; 11 (2), Agencia El Universal/Pepe Escárpita/AP Photo; 11 (3), Cara Barron/Alamy; 11 (4), Charles Phoenix; 11 (5), martiapunts/Shutterstock; 11 (6), stockcreations/Shutterstock; 11 (7), Ben Mast/Alamy; 11 (8), Tribune Content Agency LLC/Alamy; 12-13 (BACKGROUND), Mercury Press/Caters News Agency; 14 (1), Danielle Clough; 14 (2), Janne Parviainen; 14-15 (3), Barak Hardley; 15 (4), Linda Miller Nicholson of SaltySeattle; 15 (5), Jack-o-Lantern Spectacular; 15 (6), Culinary Canvas; 15 (7), Irina Pechyorina/Shutterstock; 15 (8), bankerwin/Shutterstock; 16 (1), VCG/Getty Images; 16 (2), Songquan Deng/Shutterstock; 16 (3), Claudia Beretta/agefotostock; 17 (4), DeadDuck/Getty Images; 17 (5), vichie81/Shutterstock; 17 (6), PoohFotoz/Shutterstock; 17 (7), Anne-BrittSvinnset/Getty Images; 17 (8), Brian Lawrence/Getty Images; 18 (1), Leopold Nekula/Sygma/Getty Images; 18 (2), Kenneth Garrett/Danita Delimont Photography/Newscom; 19 (3), Kenneth Garrett/National Geographic Creative; 19 (4), Matt Rourke/AP Photo; 19 (5), Gianni Dagli Orti/REX/Shutterstock; 19 (6), Design Pics Inc/National Geographic Creative; 19 (7), The Natural History Museum/Alamy; 19 (8 LE), Attila Volgyi Xinhua News Agency/Newscom; 19 (8 RT), Europics/Newscom; 20 (1), Clive Postlethwaite/Rex/Shutterstock; 20 (2), Gregory Rec/Portland Press Herald/Getty Images; 20 (3), Thomas Peter/Reuters; 21 (4), Yves Herman/Reuters; 21 (5), Michael Wheatley/Alamy; 21 (6), Woody FitzHugh; 21 (7), Mark Peterson/Redux; 21 (8), Ron Buskirk/agefotostock; 22 (1), Norbert Wu/Minden Pictures/National Geographic Creative; 23 (2), Tom McHugh/Science Source; 23 (3), Christian Ziegler/Minden Pictures/National Geographic Creative; 23 (4), Auscape/Getty Images; 23 (5), Niels van Gijn/Getty Images; 23 (6), Helen E. Grose/Dreamstime.com; 23 (7), talseN/Shutterstock; 23 (8), Augusto Leandro Stanzani/ardea.com; 24-25 (BACKGROUND), Kevin Schafer/Minden Pictures; 26 (1), John A Davis/Shutterstock; 26 (2), Nuttapong Wongcheronkit/Shutterstock; 26 (3), Zhasmina Ivanova/Dreamstime.com; 27 (4), Magrath/Folsom/Getty Images; 27 (5), jordiphotography/Alamy; 27 (6), MinervaStudio/Dreamstime.com; 27 (7), NASA/Bill Ingalls; 27 (8), NASA/Goddard Space Flight Center, The SeaWiFS Project and GeoEye, Scientific Visualization Studio; 28 (1), Brenda Carson/Shutterstock; 28 (2), Jean-Jacques Alcalay/Minden Pictures; 29 (3), Chantelle Bosch/Shutterstock; 29 (4), Rob Hainer/Shutterstock; 29 (5), PhotoBarmaley/Shutterstock; 29 (6), Kamonrat/Shutterstock; 29 (7), Brian J. Skerry/National Geographic Creative; 29 (8), Tollkÿhn/ullstein bild/Getty Images; 30 (1), Robbie Shone/National Geographic Creative; 31 (2), Aurora Photos/Alamy; 31 (3), David S. Boyer and Arlan R. Wiker/National Geographic Creative; 31 (4), Kevin Foy/REX/Shutterstock; 31 (5), Ben Lewis/Alamy; 31 (6), kurtlichtenstein/Getty Images; 31 (7), La Venta Esplorazioni Geografiche-Alessio Romeo; 31 (8), Liz Rogers Photography; 32-33 (BACKGROUND), Yann Arthus-Bertrand/Getty Images; 34 (1), Marie Appert/Shutterstock; 34 (2), Library of Congress Prints and Photographs Division, Washington, DC; 35 (3), lev radin/Shutterstock; 35 (4), epa european pressphoto agency b.v./Alamy; 35 (5), CR Shelare/Getty Images; 35 (6), VisitBritain/John Coutts/Getty Images; 35 (7), Yasuyoshi Chiba/AFP/Getty Images; 35 (8), Zuma Press Inc/Alamy; 36 (1), Nick Potts/Zuma Press/Newscom; 36 (2), Jane Herr/Featurechina/Newscom; 37 (3), Daniel Munoz/Reuters; 37 (4), Laurence Griffiths/Getty Images; 37 (5), Frank Fife/AFP/Getty Images; 37 (6), Victor Fraile/Power Sport Images/Getty Images; 37 (7), Brett Carlsen/Getty Images; 37 (8), Sport In Pictures/Alamy; 38 (1), Stuart G Porter/Shutterstock; 38 (2), Jurgen & Christine Sohns/Getty Images; 38 (3), Arco Images GmbH/Alamy; 39 (4), Jose B. Ruiz/Minden Pictures; 39 (5), Edwin Giesbers/naturepl.com; 39 (6), elitravo/Shutterstock; 39 (7), Gerard Lacz/Minden Pictures; 39 (8), Rod Williams/Minden Pictures; 40 (1), Andy Roberts/Alamy; 40 (2), Saeed Khan/AFP/Getty Images; 41 (3), Mark Metcalfe/Getty Images; 41 (4), Manfred Gottschalk/Alamy; 41 (5), Manfred Gottschalk/Alamy;41 (6), iStock Editorial/Getty Images; 41 (7), Mark Metcalfe/Getty Images;41 (8), William West/AFP/Getty Images; 42 (1), Aurora Photos/Alamy; 42 (2), North Wind Picture Archives/The Image Works; 42 (3), SWNS/Splash News/Newscom; 43 (4), Paul Hameister; 43 (5), Library of Congress Prints and Photographs Division, Washington, DC; 43 (6), Johnny Green/Photoshot/Newscom; 43 (7), Brendon Thorne/Getty Images; 43 (8), Arnaud Guerin; 44 (1), Andrey Rudenko; 45 (2), Andrew Harrer/Bloomberg via Getty Images; 45 (3), Michael Appleton/The New York Times/Redux Pictures; 45 (4), Piero Cruciatti/Alamy; 45 (5), VCG/Getty Images; 45 (6), CB2/ZOB/Supplied by WENN.com/Newscom; 45 (7), Will Ragozzino/BFA/REX/Shutterstock; 45 (8), Tobias Schwarz/AFP/Getty Images; 46-47 (BACKGROUND), Matthias Balk/dpa/picture-alliance/Newscom; 48 (1), Giulio Ercolani/Alamy; 48 (2), Aflo Co. Ltd./Alamy; 49 (3), Reuters/Alamy; 49 (4), Pochard Pascal/SIPA/Newscom; 49 (5), Hercules Milas/Alamy; 49 (6), DV Oenology/Alamy; 49 (7), CB2/ZOB/Supplied by WENN.com/Newscom; 49 (8), Santos Expre/Newscom; 50 (1), Thomas P. Peschak/National Geographic Creative; 50 (2), Nicholas Smythe/Getty Images; 51 (3), Hadot/Dreamstime.com; 51 (4), Robin Smith/Getty Images; 51 (5), Niels Poulsen DK/Alamy; 51 (6), Michael Lynch/Shutterstock; 51 (7), Shin.T/Getty Images; 51 (8), Ingrid Visser/Hedgehog House/Minden Pictures/National Geographic Creative; 52 (1), LVV/Shutterstock; 52 (2), Kagai19927/Shutterstock; 53 (3), Phil Degginger/Alamy; 53 (4), Phil Degginger/Alamy;53 (5), Albert Russ/Shutterstock; 53 (6), The Natural History Museum/The Image Works; 53 (7), Tomatito/Shutterstock; 53 (8), The Natural History Museum/The Image Works;54 (1), Kyle Huber; 54 (2), gorillaimages/Shutterstock; 54 (3), Matthew Rakola/National Geographic Kids; 55 (4), imagebroker/Alamy; 55 (5), Jorge Saenz; 55 (6), Marc Torrell; 55 (7), David Trood/Getty Images; 55 (8), Slinkachu; 56 (1), Sampics/Corbis via Getty Images; 56 (2), Jekesai Njikizana/AFP/Getty Images; 57 (3), Chung Sung-Jun/Getty Images; 57 (4), Osman Orsal/AP Photo; 57 (5), VCG/Getty Images; 57 (6), Jeff Moreland/Icon SMI/Corbis/Getty Images; 57 (7), Power Sport Images/Getty Images; 57 (8), Icon Sportswire/Getty Images; 58 (1), MyLoupe/Universal Images Group/Getty Images; 59 (2), Peter Bischoff/Getty Images; 59 (3), Yann Layma/Getty Images; 59 (4), Taylor Weidman/Getty Images; 59 (5), Carl De Souza/AFP/Getty Images; 59 (6), Ray Tang/Anadolu Agency/Getty Images; 59 (7), Reuters/Alamy; 59 (8), VCG/Getty Images; 60 (1), Goncaloferreira/Dreamstime.com; 60 (2), David Hosking/Minden Pictures; 60 (3), Tui De Roy/Minden Pictures; 61 (4), Pablo Hidalgo/Dreamstime.com; 61 (5), Jeff Mauritzen; 61 (6), Tui De Roy/Minden Pictures; 61 (7), Nyker1/Dreamstime.com; 61 (8), nouseforname/Shutterstock; 62-63 (BACKGROUND), Tui De Roy/naturepl.com; 64 (1), Ria Novosti/TopFoto/The Image Works; 64 (2), Gabriela Maj/Bloomberg/Getty Images; 64 (3), jirawatfoto/Shutterstock; 65 (4), saiko3p/Shutterstock; 65 (5), Wiskerke/Alamy; 65 (6), Alexmama/Shutterstock; 65 (7), Reuters/Alamy; 65 (8), Zack Frank/Shutterstock; 66 (1), Ben Curtis/AP Photo; 66 (2), Costume Desginer: Ami Goodheart; Photographer: Ted Sabarese; 67 (3), Ding Haitao/Xinhua/Zuma Press; 67 (4), Ozshotz/Alamy; 67 (5), Venturelli/Getty Images; 67 (6), Gene Blevins/Polaris/Newscom; 67 (7), Nancy Morries-Judd, Recycle Runway; 67 (8), Krisztian Bocsi/Bloomberg via Getty Images; 68 (1), Guy Corbishley/Alamy; 68 (2), Justin Sullivan/Getty Images; 69 (3), Jonathan Nackstrand/AFP/Getty Images; 69 (4), Morne de Klerk/Getty Images; 69 (5), Holger Hollemann/AFT/Getty Images; 69 (6), dpa picture alliance/Alamy; 69 (7), Mandel Ngana/AFP/Getty Images; 69 (8), Cameron Spencer/Getty Images; 70 (1), Brek Nebel/Caters News Agency; 70 (2), Aleksandra Djokic/Shutterstock; 70 (3), Jessica Siskin; 71 (4), Fresheather; 71 (5), usako/Shutterstock; 71 (6), PP_photography/Shutterstock; 71 (7), David Laferriere; 71 (8), Tama-Chan, Simiiing Sushi Roll; 72 (1), Photo Insolite Realite/Science Photo Library/Getty Images; 72 (2), Scott Camazine/Science Source; 73 (3), Photo Insolite Realite/Science Photo Library/Getty Images; 73 (4), Visuals Unlimited, Inc./Science VU/Dr. Merton Brown/Getty Images; 73 (5), Dennis Kunkel Microscopy/Science Source; 73 (6), Studio29ro/Dreamstime.com; 73 (7), Visuals Unlimited, Inc./Dr. Stanley Flegler/Getty Images; 73 (8), Stegerphoto/Getty Images; 74 (1), Zbiq/Shutterstock; 75 (2), Wojtek Buss/Getty Images; 75 (3), Cesar Manso/AFP/Getty Images; 75 (4), Pius Lee/Shutterstock; 75 (5), AF archive/Alamy; 75 (6), Regissercom/Shutterstock; 75 (7), Science History Images/Alamy; 75 (8), Vicky Jirayu/Shutterstock; 76-77 (BACKGROUND), Richard Cummins/Getty Images; 78 (1), Justin Goff/UK Press via Getty Images; 78 (2), Thomas Woodruff/Dreamstime.com; 78 (3), Patrick Lynch Photography/Shutterstock; 79 (4), Jean-Christophe Verhaegen/AFP/Getty Images; 79 (5), Ritu Manoj Jethani/Shutterstock; 79 (6), Berbar Halim/SIPA/Newscom; 79 (7), Marcos Delgado/Clasos.com/LatinContent/Getty Images; 79 (8), stepmorem/Shutterstock; 80 (1), Chris Mattison/agefotostock; 80 (2), Buena Vista Images/Getty Images; 81 (3), AlexmarPhoto/iStock/Getty Images; 81 (4), Stefan Auth imagebroker/Newscom; 81 (5), Yai_Goes/iStock/Getty Images; 81 (6), Michael Nichols/National Geographic Creative; 81 (7), Gil.K/Shutterstock; 81 (8), Noradoa/Shutterstock; 82 (1), Robert Mora/Getty Images; 82 (2), Christopher Morris/Zuma Press/Newscom; 82 (3), JVT/Getty Images; 83 (4), ohrim/Shutterstock; 83 (5), Clement Mahoudeau/IP/Getty Images; 83 (6), Don Bartletti/Los Angeles Times/Getty Images; 83 (7), Mathieu Belanger/The New York Times/Redux Pictures; 83 (8), Daniel Milchev/Getty Images; 84 (1), Patrick Demazeau; 84 (2), Maximo Riera Studio; 85 (3), Caters News Agency; 85 (4), Jessica Bolin, Big Things Small Town; 85 (5), Hugh Threlfall/Alamy; 85 (6), davide piras/Alamy; 85 (7), Radharc Images/Alamy; 85 (8), Geraint Lewis/Alamy; 86 (1), Kelvin Aitken/VWPics/Alamy; 86 (2), D. R. Schrichte/SeaPics.com; 87 (3), Science Source; 87 (4), Science Source;87 (5), Steve Downer/ardea.com; 87 (6), David Doubilet/National Geographic Creative; 87 (7), NHPA/Photoshot; 87 (8), D. R. Schrichte/SeaPics.com; 88 (1), NASA, ESA, and the Hubble Heritage Team (STScI/AURA); 89 (2), NASA/JHUAPL/SwRI; 89 (3), Babak Tafreshi/National Geographic Creative; 89 (4), NASA/SSPL/The Image Works; 89 (5), Lynette Cook/Science Source; 89 (6), NASA/Ames/JPL-Caltech; 89 (7), NASA Photo/Alamy; 89 (8), NASA/JPL/Space Science Institute; 90-91 (BACKGROUND), Detlev van Ravenswaay/Getty Images; 92 (1), Nazzu/Shutterstock; 92 (2), Paul Sawer/FLPA; 92 (3), Zachary Fabian/Dreamstime.com; 93 (4), Jesse Nguyen/Shutterstock; 93 (5), Tim Laman/National Geographic Creative; 93 (6), Lukas Blazek/Dreamstime.com; 93 (7), All Canada Photos/Alamy; 93 (8), Eky Studio/Shutterstock; 94 (1), Keystone View Co/National Geographic Stock; 94 (2), NASA; 95 (3), Peter Newark American Pictures/Bridgeman Images; 95 (4), Hong Nian Zhang/National Geographic Creative; 95 (5), Frank Hurley/Scott Polar Research Institute, University of Cambridge/Getty Images; 95 (6), Look and Learn/Bridgeman Images; 95 (7), Photo Ken Welsh/Bridgeman Images; 95 (8), Interphoto/Alamy; 96 (1), Fred Dufour/AFP/Getty Images; 96 (2), Reuters/Yves Herman; 96 (3), Caters News Agency; 97 (4), Four Seasons Resorts Mauritius at Anahita/Photographer: Ken Seet; 97 (5), Longitude 131; 97 (6), Sublimotion Ibiza; 97 (7), Scott Wright of Limelight Studio; 97 (8), Four Seasons Budapest; 98-99, Franco Tempesta; 100 (1), Jedediah Volts, photo by Sean Plew; 100 (2), Althea Crome/Caters News Agency; 100 (3), Jon Almeda; 101 (4), Willard Wigan; 101 (5), Hoang Tran; 101 (6), Stéphanie Kilgast; 101 (7), Brooke Rothshank; 101 (8), Slinkachu; 102 (1), Maarten de Boer/Getty Images; 103 (2), Johnny Haglund/Getty Images; 103 (3), Abeselom Zerit/Dreamstime.com; 103 (4), James L. Stanfield/National Geographic Creative; 103 (5), theskaman306/Shutterstock; 103 (6), David Edwards/National Geographic Creative; 103 (7), Wolfgang Zwanzger/Shutterstock; 103 (8), Francois Gohier/Science Source; 104 (1), David J Slater/Alamy; 104 (2), KeithSzafranski/iStock; 104 (3), ZSSD/Minden Pictures; 105 (4), Kitchin & Hurst/KimballStock; 105 (5), Design Pics Inc/Alamy; 105 (6), Keren Su/China Span/Alamy; 105 (7), Jean-Paul Ferrero/ardea.com; 105 (8), Suzi Eszterhas/Minden Pictures; 106 (1), Nick Ledger/Getty Images; 106 (2), Westend61/Getty Images; 107 (3), TommL/Getty Images; 107 (4), Aaron Lim/Shutterstock; 107 (5), kropic1/Shutterstock; 107 (6), William Perugini/Shutterstock; 107 (7), Dove Lee/Getty Images; 107 (8), Igor Plotnikov/Shutterstock; 108 (1), taweesak thiprod/Shutterstock; 108 (2), Mark Lewis/Getty Images; 109 (3), Douglas Peebles Photography/Alamy; 109 (4), Pascal Kobeh/Minden Pictures; 109 (5), Michael Melford/National Geographic Creative; 109 (6), Raul Touzon/National Geographic Creative; 109 (7), Stephen Dalton/Minden Pictures; 109 (8), m-kojot/Getty Images; 112, Robert Eastman/Shutterstock

LEAVING SO SOON?
HERE IS A QUICK LIGHTNING LIST TO KEEP THE FUN GOING:

EIGHT
COOL WAYS TO SAY
GOODBYE

1. LET'S MAKE LIKE A BANANA AND SPLIT.
2. I'VE GOT TO MAKE LIKE A TREE AND LEAVE.
3. SEE YOU LATER, ALLIGATOR!
4. LET'S MAKE LIKE AN AIRPLANE AND TAKE OFF.
5. IT'S TIME FOR ME TO MAKE LIKE LIGHTNING AND BOLT!
6. I SHOULD MAKE LIKE A JACKET AND ZIP.
7. LET'S MAKE LIKE A CAR AND HIT THE ROAD.
8. WE'VE GOT TO MAKE LIKE A BALL AND BOUNCE.

Copyright © 2018 National Geographic Partners, LLC

Published by National Geographic Partners, LLC.
All rights reserved. Reproduction of the whole or any part of the contents without written permission from the publisher is prohibited.

Since 1888, the National Geographic Society has funded more than 12,000 research, exploration, and preservation projects around the world. The Society receives funds from National Geographic Partners, LLC, funded in part by your purchase. A portion of the proceeds from this book supports this vital work. To learn more, visit natgeo.com/info.

NATIONAL GEOGRAPHIC and Yellow Border Design are trademarks of the National Geographic Society, used under license.

For more information, visit nationalgeographic.com, call 1-800-647-5463, or write to the following address:

National Geographic Partners
1145 17th Street N.W.
Washington, D.C. 20036-4688 U.S.A.

Visit us online at nationalgeographic.com/books

For librarians and teachers: ngchildrensbooks.org

More for kids from National Geographic: natgeokids.com

For information about special discounts for bulk purchases, please contact National Geographic Books Special Sales: specialsales@natgeo.com

For rights or permissions inquiries, please contact National Geographic Books Subsidiary Rights: bookrights@natgeo.com

Designed by Nicole Lazarus

Trade paperback ISBN: 978-1-4263-3006-3
Reinforced library binding ISBN: 978-1-4263-3007-0

The publisher would like to acknowledge Julie Beer, Michelle Harris, Jen Agresta, Michaela Weglinski, Danny Meldung, Lori Epstein, Nicole Lazarus, Sanjida Rashid, Joan Gossett, Anne LeongSon, and Gus Tello.

Printed in China
18/RRDS/1